the
Signature
of
Jesus

Books by Brennan Manning

Lion and Lamb
Stranger to Self-Hatred
The Gentle Revolutionaries
The Wisdom of Accepted Tenderness
Prophets and Lovers
Souvenirs of Solitude

the Signature of Jesus

BRENNAN MANNING

Published by
√ chosen books

FLEMING H. REVELL COMPANY
OLD TAPPAN, NEW JERSEY

Scripture quotations are from:
  The King James Version of the Bible.
  The New American Standard Bible, copyright © The Lockman Foundation
1960, 1962, 1963, 1968, 1971, 1972, 1973, 1975, 1977.
  The Holy Bible, New International Version, copyright © 1978 by the Interna-
tional Bible Society, used by permission of Zondervan Bible Publishers.
  The Jerusalem Bible, copyright © 1966 by Darton, Longman & Todd, Ltd., and
Doubleday & Company, Inc.

Library of Congress Cataloging-in-Publication Data
Manning, Brennan.
  The signature of Jesus.

  "Chosen books."
  Includes bibliographies.
  1. Christian life—1960–   . 2. Jesus Christ—
Person and offices. I. Title.
BV4501.2.M3376   1988   248.4   87–28843
ISBN 0-8007-9128-2

A Chosen Book
Copyright © 1988 by Brennan Manning
Chosen Books are published by
Fleming H. Revell Company
Old Tappan, New Jersey
Printed in the United States of America

For Paul and Jenny Sheldon,
steadfast friends, who stood
with Roslyn and me in
the bad weather of life.

Contents

Foreword. 9

One
The Discipline of the Secret 13

Two
The Signature of Jesus. 36

Three
Fools for Christ 50

Four
Discipleship Today 65

Five
Paschal Spirituality 85

Six
Celebrate the Darkness 104

Seven
The Love of Jesus 120

Eight
The Dimensions of the Dragnet. 141

Contents

Nine
The Courage to Risk....................................157

Ten
The Time to Pray.......................................167

Eleven
Lazarus Laughed! 173

Epilogue 180

Notes 185

Foreword

This book is a good sermon by a man who burns to tell the church what he thinks its people need to hear. Brennan Manning is a story-teller, and his stories tell the story of his love-hate relationship with God's ecclesia. His ambivalence stems from his keen awareness that the Church, on the one hand, has trivialized the Gospel and, on the other hand, is still the Body of Christ, apart from which there's no salvation. Manning puts into words the groanings that many of us feel when we are faced with the abuses of the narcissistic religiosity so evident these days on the American scene. But his feelings remind us that this messed-up Church is still a Church that is loved by the Lord.

As I read his book, I realized how much this man is still in process. He lets us peek into his life as he gives us hints of where he has been and what he has done on his spiritual journey. We follow him from his conversion from suicidal alcoholism into the priestly ministry of the Church. He gives us a taste of his venture into the desert. In solitary devotion, he searched his soul and tried to get in touch with God. He invites us to understand the mystical leading that gave him the sense of "rightness" that he felt when he left the pastorate of Roman Catholicism and entered into marriage with his wife, Roslyn. Everything he tells me blesses and helps me. But, by the end of the book, I had a sense that his journey was just beginning. Furthermore, I had an inkling as to where he might be going in the years to come. Unconsciously, he provides signposts pointing to his future and where he might be taking me when he writes again.

It is quite clear that Manning, for all of his devotional tone and personalistic style, has a concern for societal issues. As a matter of fact, I felt that his attack on the Church's tendency to become preoccupied with petty and trivial issues comes from his frustration over the failure of the Church to deal with the crucial concerns of our world. He is close to being prophetic when he condemns nuclear arms (but then, who doesn't condemn the arms race?). I wish, however, that he had gone on to take a stand as to what we should do about it. I wish that he had been specific and said something about the "Star Wars" progam as it relates to Christian stewardshp. I would have liked it if he had addressed the power plays of the United States in Central America and called for repentance by those who arrogantly impose their will on others. Of course, taking such stands is risky and could get Manning crucified. But then, taking risks and getting crucified is "the signature of Jesus," which is what the book is all about.

When it comes to discipleship, Manning rails against the "cheap grace" so eloquently condemned by Detrich Bonhoeffer. He clearly delineates the fact that Christians are to have the fanatical commitment of revolutionaries rather than their lukewarm styles of Church life. His anger over the ways in which discipleship has been watered down by the Church in an effort to broaden its appeal and maximize its membership is important for us to hear. However, I think that in the future his call to discipleship will be for an even more radical commitment to the lifestyle prescribed in the Sermon on the Mount. Brennan does not yet spell out the strenuous requirements of the biblically prescribed simple life so effectively lived out by St. Francis. But I sense that he is on the way to the radical stance of the medieval mode.

Strict adherence to the message of Jesus raises serious questions about those of us who subscribe to the affluent American lifestyle while our brothers and sisters in Third World countries suffer because their basic needs go unmet. Manning's call to radical obedience to the commands of our Lord must lead to a willingness to live simply that others may simply live. We all carry too much culturally prescribed baggage to call ourselves true Christians. It is difficult to discern that we are disciples of the One who told those who would follow Him to unpackage their lives, sell all, give to the poor, deny themselves, and take up the cross. We are far from being a people who "take no thought for tomorrow," giving no thought to what we will eat and what we will wear. Indeed, we are those Gentiles who seek after such things. We are not like the easy riders described in the tenth chapter of Matthew, who traveled light and picked up what they needed along the way. We are people who have gotten bogged down in surburbia. Brennan is one of us, and he does not pretend to be otherwise. And yet, I detect in this reluctant radical certain tendencies that may soon put him out in front of the rest of us pilgrims and make him into a Pauline-like figure who will be able to say, "Follow me as I follow Christ." As a Protestant reader of this Roman Catholic brother, I sense him inviting me to join him as he moves toward a lifestyle that is more like Mother Teresa's and less like Jim Bakker's.

Lastly, there is Brennan's doctrine of salvation. He holds fast to the Roman Catholic doctrines about who is saved and who is not. There is, however, too much Barthian theology in his message for him to maintain consistency. He argues strongly that he is not a universalist (and I think he doth protest too much) and yet there is a broadness in his doctrine of salvation that is too close to universalism for the comfort of those who believe in "The Great Divorce" of the just and the unjust.

On the one hand, he would carry us Protestants beyond the confines of the fundmentalism that limits salvation only to those who accept the propositional truths of Scripture that explain what Jesus did for us on the cross. He would have us buy into that Roman Catholic doctrine that the salvation of God also includes others "who are not of this fold," but who sincerely seek lives of rectitude as they follow the dictates of their consciences.

Evangelical-type Protestants have a problem with this kind of thinking. We are much more into original sin than is Manning, who, by his own admission, sees people as basically good. Calvinists, who dominate evangelism, and Pentecostals, who are running a close second these days, contend that all people are totally depraved. To accept Manning's Catholicism would appear to them to be getting into a system of salvation by works. Evangelical Protestants would read Manning as saying that even if you don't accept Jesus as savior, you can still be saved, if you work real hard at believing whatever it is you believe in and are sincere about it. "It's by grace that we are saved," scream evangelicals, "not of works, lest anyone should boast."

However, Brennan Manning will not be so easily boxed in. Just when we evanglicals are about to conclude that this Catholic brother would do well to learn something more about grace from his Protestant friends, he turns around and outdoes us at our own game. In a section of his book, which starts off with a wonderful quote from the writings of the Russian novelist, Dostoyevsky, Manning demonstrates full well that he knows what grace is all about, and does so even better than most of us. He quotes Dostoyevsky as he writes:

> At the last judgment Christ will say to us, "Come you also! Come drunkards! Come, weaklings! Come, children of shame!" And he will say to us: "Vile beings, you are in the image of the beast and bear his mark, but come all the same, you as well!" And the wise and prudent will say, "Lord, why do you welcome them?" And he will say, "If I welcome them, you wise men, if I welcome them, you prudent men, it is because not one of them has ever been judged worthy." And he will stretch out his arms,

and we will fall at his feet, and we will cry out, sobbing, and then we will understand all, we will understand the gospel of grace! "Lord, your kingdom come!"

Which is the real Manning? Is salvation only for those who, while they do not buy into our theology, sincerely seek to live lives of rectitude by obeying their consciences? Or is it also for drunkards, weaklings, and children of shame who are in the image of the beast? I think I know where Manning's heart lies, and I think I know where it will lead him—eventually. Having himself experienced the grace of God, when he knew he deserved only condemnation, he finds it difficult to limit grace to those who fall within the confines set by Canon Law. He wants to be faithful to his church, but I sense his gut feelings would make him broader. I am sure that Manning is being honest when he says that he believes in hell, but I do not believe that he believes that there are many people in it. As I suggested, Manning is an honest man and as a consequence of this honesty, he reveals with clarity the ambiguities and ambivalence of his thinking.

This is a book worth reading. It tells the old, old story with wonderful stories and makes the old, old story a new story for us all. For those of us who are on a journey and have not yet arrived, the markings left by this fellow traveler are worth noting. They can help us. But, let there be warning. The path suggested by Brennan Manning will lead us to a cross and require that we die to ourselves: that is—if we want to write with the signature of Jesus.

Dr. Anthony Campolo
St. David's, Pennsylvania

One

The Discipline
of the Secret

Christian imagination, rooted in Jesus and anchored in
His Word, is neither old ice cream nor tame sausage.
It avoids the unrestrained excesses of sheer fantasy and
functions in conformity to revealed truth. It also unglues
us from the status quo. In the words of David Baily
Harned, "Imagination is the sum of all the resources
within us that we employ to form accurate images of the
self and its world. The imagination is concerned with the
discovery of potentiality and new possibilities, with what
is not yet, but only because it is oriented first of all toward
actuality."[1]

Grounded in the solid foundation of the Gospel, Christian imagination liberates us from the tyranny of existing
arrangements, opens up new ways of looking at the
world, Church, and self, holds out the wild possibility that

I can be more than I am at any given moment, and suggests that the epitaph on my tombstone will read more than: "He muttered prayers, mowed his lawn, and lost a thousand golf balls."

This past year my ministry as a wandering evangelist has taken me from the National Prayer Breakfast in the Washington Hilton to a remote hermitage in the Colorado mountains, from door-to-door evangelism in the second-poorest county in the country (Nelson County, Virginia) to one thousand affluent college students in Santa Barbara, California. I have preached the Gospel in Durham, New Hampshire; Seattle, Washington; Salt Lake City, Utah; Orlando, Florida; and countless places in-between. Through my travels I am exposed to a wide spectrum of Christian communities. Frequently, I was asked, "Brennan, what do you see happening in the American Church?" In response to that question, I invite you to join me on a journey in Christian imagination.

For a moment let's imagine that the apostle Paul has been given a crash course in the English language and contemporary American idioms and transported in a time machine into the present. . . .

It was Sunday morning. Paul wandered down the main thoroughfare of a well-scrubbed suburb and inquired of a resident waxing his BMW where the Christian community was gathering for worship.

The bemused man replied: "Well, that depends whether you're into charismatic, evangelical, mainline, nondenominational, rock, Pentecostal, or electronic church."

A bewildered Paul said, "Just the nearest one."

"Right there on the corner," the man pointed.

As Paul entered the Gothic-style structure, he was handed a bulletin by an unspeaking usher. Surprised by the sparse number of worshipers, Paul took a seat, opened the bulletin and read: "To make it convenient for everyone to attend church next week, we are going to have a special

'No Excuse Sunday.' Cots will be provided in the foyer for those who say, 'Sunday is my only day to sleep in.'

"We will have steel helmets for those who say, 'The roof would cave in if I ever came to church.' Blankets will be provided for those who find it too cold, and fans for those for whom it is too hot. We will have hearing aids for those for whom the priest speaks too softly, and cotton balls for those who feel he preaches too loudly. Scorecards will be provided for those who wish to list the hypocrites present.

"Relatives will be in attendance for those who like to visit the family on Sundays. There will be TV dinners for those who can't go to church and cook dinner too. One section of the sanctuary will be planted in trees and grass for those who like to see God in nature. Finally, the altar will be decorated with both Christmas poinsettias and Easter lilies for those who have never seen the church without them. Please tell your friends about this special Sunday and reassure the health-conscious that no one has ever contracted AIDS in this building."[2]

The thunderous peal of the organ jolted Paul from his reading as the service began. After a perfunctory prayer by the celebrant, Paul's heart quickened to the story of the cleansing of the Temple from John's Gospel. Mechanically, the congregation sat back down and the sermon began:

"My brothers and sisters, on this sun-drenched Sunday morning we come together to weep and mourn. Why? Because we live in an illiterate country. The mass media pander to the lowest of the low in human experience. They debase us through the sheer weight of their mind-lessness. They would have us believe that all Protestant evangelists are adulterers and all Catholic priests are homosexuals. I vigorously dispute their sweeping indictments.

"However, we cannot ignore the perversity of the 'name it and claim it' gospel—the school of Christian thought stressing the belief that God rewards faith with material blessings. This past week when I saw the son of a famous televangelist urge viewers to help his father raise eight million dollars by sowing a seed on their Master-Card, Visa, or American Express, expecting God in return to open the windows of heaven and pour out a blessing, I was indignant. The father's latest gimmick, in case you don't know, was to mail out a million plastic bags filled with holy water from his 'River of Life' fountain. Then, when on national television he demonstrated the elixir's use by anointing his own wallet with the miraculous liquid, I was plumb-flat appalled. Small wonder that according to the latest Gallup poll, sixty-three percent of Americans regard TV preachers as untrustworthy.

"This morning's Gospel tells us that Christ drove the moneychangers from the Temple. Those Temple peddlers were nickel-and-dimers compared to our present-day TV charlatans who wheel and deal in millions. Are they saving souls or their ministries? Don't you sometimes wonder why God doesn't do something about getting rid of all these so-called ministries? Perhaps He could grant some common sense to their supporters who send in money. Then TV evangelism would dry up and blow away. Praise the Lord!

"My brothers and sisters, as you well know, I am not like these money-grubbers. In the words of Paul the apostle, 'I do not go around offering the Word of God for sale, as many other people do.' I do not own a $1.2 million home in North Carolina or drive a $55,000 Rolls Royce. Nevertheless, this morning I gotta ask you for money. The Pope is coming in three months and there's no point kidding ourselves. Big bucks or, if you prefer, major coin is involved. Our diocese is committed for $3 million. We need a special 100-foot crucifix along with 200 imported palm trees on St. Philomena Avenue. The land-scaping alone goes for $200,000. And don't forget the small river to be built for the Mass in the Dome. It's a perfect replica of the Grand Canyon in Phoenix. The $11,000 set of Noritake china for the papal meals has already been donated by a generous benefactor, thank God, but we want to reimburse Gourmet Restaurants, Inc., for the nine catered meals. I urge you to dig deep, for nothing is too elaborate for the servant of the servants of God. Allow me to make a couple of practical suggestions. Maybe you have a life insurance policy worth $5,000. One anonymous donor contributed 30 china plates embossed with Norman Rockwell illustrations valued at $1,500. As our beloved brother Paul says: 'God loves a cheerful giver.'

"And now, my friends, let us stand and pray for the holy Church of God. . . ." At that moment the microphone in the pulpit went dead. The priest tapped it gently with no result. Leaning close to it, he muttered, "There's something wrong with this microphone."

And the well-trained congregation responded, "And also with you."

Paul left the church in deep dismay. Stomach churning, he decided to follow his own advice to Timothy and purchased a California wine cooler from a street vendor. Across the street a spacious park beckoned. Paul seated himself next to an elderly gentleman feeding the pigeons. "Excuse me, sir, but could you give me your perspective on the state of the Christian community in the United States today?"[3]

The man turned and appraised Paul. What he saw was a man of small stature with a large nose, sparse red hair, gray eyes under thick joined eyebrows, and a heavy beard. Who was he? A dilettante dabbling in spiritual things? An empty-headed media mole digging for dirt? The enemy disguised as an angel of light? None of the above? "Why do you ask?"

"Because life for me means Christ," Paul answered, "and the Church is the living Jesus extended in time and space. If people are to encounter Christ today, they must find Him in His members, His Body, the Christian community. My friend, there is only Christ and He is everything and in everything."

The older man clad in jeans, a turtleneck, and Reeboks listened intently, his eyes never leaving Paul's face. *This inconspicuous little Jew emanates an unquestionable spiritual force*, he thought. But his appearance, his gestures, his voice did not fit the conventional picture of piety. He seemed neither worldly nor mystical, but there was something in his eyes that authenticated the words he spoke. It wasn't that riveting, unflinching gaze suggesting a slightly neurotic condition masquerading as religious intensity. This passionate little Jew wasn't trying to convince himself or convert anyone else with one sledgehammer blow of the Bible after another. *I have met farmers*, the old man thought, *farmers who talked with unfeigned enthusiasm about their potato crop. And I have met preachers and teachers apparently on fire who have mesmerized me with spellbinding oratory interlaced with humor and calculated self-disclosure, but there was something in their eyes that gave them away. A barely perceptible movement of the eyes revealed that the speaker inhabited a vacant part of his mind. He had polished and repolished his style for years, until he came to forget completely the substance and spoke merely for the sake of speaking. Our eyes betray us and contradict our rhetoric. The farmers were more credible. It's all in the eyes.*

"Let's take a walk, Mister . . . ?"

"My name is Paul. And yours?"

"Daniel. My brother, there has never been a time in the history of Christianity when the name of Jesus Christ is so frequently mentioned and the content of His life and teaching so thoroughly ignored. The words of Jesus have been twisted, spindled, and mutilated to mean everything, anything, and nothing. The seduction of counterfeit discipleship has made it too easy to be a Christian.

"On the academic side, the professors of religion have turned Christianity into the religion of the professors. They speak to one another in pedantic language about the soteriological value of Jesus' death. They write learned papers in dreary prose, pursue with utmost finesse the exegesis of a Gospel passage, split hairs over hermeneutical principles, and seldom if ever relate the Word of God to the needs of the contemporary Christian community. Study of the Scriptures substitutes for creative Christian conduct.

"What Martin Luther and the other Reformers learned from the apostle Paul, 'To know nothing except Jesus Christ and Him crucified,' has been forgotten. By and large today, American Christians are spoonfed on the pablum of popular religion. Morality tinged with emotion is the staple of the Sunday sermon. When the rapport between clergy and laity is one of mutual admiration, gutsy, uncompromising Christianity dissolves into verbal Alka-Seltzer and prophetic preaching becomes virtually impossible.

"When the Gospel is preached with purity and power, it should force us to reassess the entire direction of our lives. The Word breaks our train of thought, cracks open our capsuled doctrine, shatters our life of comfortable piety and well-fed virtue. The flashing spirit of Jesus breaks new paths everywhere. The Gospel is no Pollyanna tale for the neutral but a cutting knife, rolling thunder, convulsive earthquake in the world of the human spirit. As I said a moment ago, Paul, we have made it too easy today to be a Christian. In the words of Dietrich Bonhoeffer, many Christians 'have gathered like ravens around the carcass of cheap grace and there have drunk the poison which has killed the life of following Christ.'

"If the Gospel were proclaimed without compromise, the roster of card-carrying Christians would shrink considerably. Therein lies the success of televangelism. These programs distort the Gospel. There is no reference to the Cross except as a theological relic, no clarion call to the Body of Christ that we are crucified to the world and the world to us. In a half hour the electronic evangelist has to convert you, which trivializes what conversion means, heal you, which is hokey, and guarantee your success. Everybody is a winner; nobody loses his business, fails in marriage, or lives in poverty. If you are an attractive nineteen-year-old and accept Jesus, you become Miss America; if you have a drinking problem you conquer alcoholism; if you play in the National Football League, you go automatically to the Pro Bowl.

"On a recent Phil Donahue program, a woman stated that out of her total monthly income of $238 from a Social Security check, she sent $45 to a television ministry. The money was squandered by the evangelists on personal extravagances. After the couple was exposed and disgraced, they returned from their sumptuous villa in the far West to their native state. *Newsweek* magazine described their triumphal return this way: 'Ecstatic followers compared it to the entry of Christ into Jerusalem.'

"How is such absurdity possible? What has happened that the Word of Jesus can thus be degraded and left open to the mockery of the world?[4]

"Yet, brother Paul, a far more egregious error is bewitching God's people across the land." The two men were strolling along a gravel path. "This is the insidious temptation to give a monopoly on evil to a single nation like the Soviet Union, or a single institution like the Roman Catholic Church or a single individual like a greedy televangelist.

"When one person, group, or organization is declared Satan, the source of all evil, then naturally if we put out a contract on that source and blow it away—bam, slam, whoppo, right in the kisser—then everything will be all right. When Satan is localized in a finite reality, the end of evil seems in sight. Eliminate this one thing and paradise will be restored. Utopia is around the corner. And because of the crucial importance of this crusade, it must be a no-holds-barred, damn-the-torpedoes, full-speed-ahead onslaught. The success of such a campaign is more frightening to me than its failure.

"One lesson we learn from history is that when people kill their 'Satan,' they soon notice that evil has not disappeared from the face of the earth. In fact, it reappears in the place they least suspect—themselves. In the movie *Ben Hur*, when Judah has finally killed his archenemy Massala, Judah's lover says to him, 'It is as if you have become Massala.' The same theme was explored in the recent film *The Star Chamber*. Outraged at the inequities of the criminal justice system, Michael Douglas joins a self-appointed group of judges who review unfair court acquittals, render their own verdict of guilty, and hire a 'hit man' to carry out the assassination. An uneasy Douglas comments, 'I have the feeling that we have become them.'

"Labeling someone Satan gets the labeler off the hook. The source of evil now has a definable shape and it is definitely not myself. The speck in the eye of another has been discerned. There is no need to look any further. We can stop focusing on the inroads that evil has made in our own hearts, nations, and institutions.

"Everyone has his pet enemy, his favorite target, his 'what's wrong with the world' speech. The villain may be the worldliness of the Church, capitalism, Communism, sexism, racism, the welfare system. For me right now, it happens to be televangelists. But instead of fulminating in self-righteous indignation against the greed of others, the Gospel calls me to make a searching moral inventory of the creeping tendency to materialism, avarice, and financial anxiety in my own life. The Master said: 'Hypocrite! Take the plank out of your own eye first, and then you will see clearly enough to take the splinter out of your brother's eye.'

"The words of Jesus in Matthew 23 are scorching ones:

'Alas for you scribes and Pharisees, you hypocrites! You who are like whitewashed tombs that look handsome on the outside, but inside are full of dead men's bones and every kind of corruption. In the same way you appear to people from the outside like good honest men, but inside you are full of hypocrisy and lawlessness.'

"Today, Paul, American Christians revel in this kind of declamation. But the tragedy is that these fierce words of Jesus are directed against others—usually contemporary authority figures in the Church. The phrases are leveled at televangelists, the Pope, bishops, our pastors. And of course we are missing Jesus' point entirely when we use His words as weapons against anyone other than ourselves. They are to be taken personally by each of us, or else they become perverted. This is the form, shape, and stuff of Christian Pharisaism today. Hypocrisy is not the prerogative of people in high places. The most impoverished among us is capable of it. Hypocrisy is the natural expression of what is meanest in us all."[5]

Daniel fell silent. Throughout his discourse he had been aware of the intensity of Paul's listening. It was not forced concentration with a knitting of the brows but the quietness of pure attention. Unclouded by the egotistical need to upstage Daniel with a display of his own wisdom, Paul's mind seemed to absorb every word he said. *There is an extraordinary quality of openness about this man*, Daniel mused, *that I do not fully understand.*

The two men sat down on a grassy knoll overlooking Lake Harmony. After twenty full minutes of silence, Paul said, "Faith comes through hearing. Are people today not hearing the Word of God?"

"Incredible as it sounds," Daniel replied, "the Word has become a source of division, estrangement, complacent piety, and intolerable self-righteousness. Last summer a prominent Pentecostal preacher refused to attend the Congress on World Evangelization in New Orleans. His primary objection was the participation of Catholics. In his own words: 'There is absolutely no way that ministers of the Gospel can stand on a platform with Catholic priests in some type of professed unity without compromising the message of the Word of God.'

"The supreme irony is that ministers of the Gospel twist the Word into the gospel of the ministers. Jesus said that the sole measure of discipleship was whether we loved one another as He has loved us. His teaching was unequivocal here: We would be known as His followers not because we are churchgoing, Bible-toting Psalm-singers but because of our deep and delicate respect for one another, our cordial love impregnated with respect for the sacred dimension of human personality.

"In an arrogant gesture of one-upmanship, many preachers have decided that Jesus' standard is inadequate for modern times. The new criterion is orthodoxy of doctrine coupled with the way we interpret the Bible. A Christian's right thinking is the new norm for determining what he or she is worth. All vices can be forgiven from gross moral lapses to spiritual indifference; what is unforgivable is deviation from doctrine and incorrect biblical interpretation. Although the Gospels themselves are minimally credal and nowhere obsessed with right beliefs and wrong beliefs, today we do not shrink from splitting up fellowships, churches, and even denominations over the form of our worship, the songs we sing, or the method of interpreting a biblical passage.

"We unleash public anger on those who do not read the Bible the way we do or honor our traditions or agree with our so-called facts. Throughout the New Testament Jesus Himself is the only fact that counts; all the others are candles lighting up this one. Today there are so many doctrinal candles burning that His light can barely be seen above them.

"Even more distressing in our Christian culture today,

Paul, is what can only be described as an idolatry of the Scriptures. For many Christians today, the Bible is not a pointer to God, but God Himself. I am weary of the God who is cribbed, cabined, and confined within the covers of a leather-bound book. I develop a nasty rash around people who speak as if mere scrutiny of its pages will reveal precisely how God thinks and precisely what God wants in every perplexity.

"The Gospels are the key to knowing Jesus. But conversely, Jesus is the key to knowing the meaning of the Gospels—and of the Bible as a whole. Instead of remaining content with the bare letter, we should pass on to the more profound mysteries that are available only through intimate heartfelt knowledge of the Person of Jesus.[6]

"For example, the recorded ruling of Jesus on the indissolubility of marriage is unbending and rigorous, without qualification. Yet, the apostle Paul, who understood the mind of Christ better than any man or woman who has ever lived, did not hesitate to intervene in the case of a believer married to an unbeliever. Invoking his own apostolic authority, based on intimacy with Jesus as well as with Jesus' words, Paul modified the Master's teaching and dissolved the marriage because 'God has called us to a life of peace.'

"The only effective foundation for Christian renewal lies in attaining Christ-consciousness, in moving beyond the letter to achieve the God-centeredness of Jesus. Failure to have the mind of Christ is the major cause of division and darkness in the American Church. We have settled for our various sets of doctrinal beliefs rather than the actual faith-experience of the risen Jesus. The result is a religion *about* Jesus and not the religion *of* Jesus.

"The violence with which people expound their beliefs betrays an attempt to convince themselves that they really do believe. The spectre of our actual belief can be so frightening that we brutally impose our beliefs on others rather than simply, peacefully living them ourselves. Whenever this fear of our own unbelief grips the churches, then what should be joyful, tolerant, and compassionate communities become pompous agents of repression. With only a mastery of biblical chapter and verse, lacking a personal knowledge of the mind of Christ, the Christian becomes a travel agent handing out brochures to places he has never visited.[7]

"The consequences of this ignorance for the spiritual life of the Church have been devastating. American Christians pay lipservice to the Gospel of grace but live under the bondage of law. How else do we explain the unhealthy guilt and self-condemnation so characteristic of Christians in this country? The National Guild of Christian Psychiatrists reported recently on the widespread phenomenon of clients tormented by intense feelings of guilt, shame, remorse, and self-hatred. It is the dominant spiritual sickness crippling American Christians and stifling their growth in the Holy Spirit. They would never dare judge other people with the savage self-condemnation with which they crush themselves.

"American spirituality starts with self, not with God. Personal responsibility replaces personal response. We are all engrossed in our own efforts to be godly. It's the Horatio Alger legend of the self-made man transferred from the economic sphere into our relationship with the Lord. God is reduced to a benign old spectator sitting in the bleachers and applauding when we manage to get to church on Sunday. Spiritual growth is attributed to our own vigorous efforts.

"When Martin Luther discovered that God, for the sake of His Son Jesus, *made* sinners righteous through the forgiveness of sins, he said it was as though the very gates of Paradise had been opened for him. In the depths of his soul he resonated to Paul's teaching in Romans on amazing grace. But Paul had the mind of Christ.

"The God-centric teaching of Jesus is paid lip service in order to safeguard orthodoxy. The typical Sunday sermon opens with a light volley on the subject of God's love. 'His love is always there waiting patiently for us. We need only to turn to Him to receive it.' Then comes the heavy artillery of legalism, moralism, perfectionism, rule-keeping, and guilt-tripping. Charges of heresy and blasphemy are hurled at Fyodor Dostoyevsky because he wrote: 'At the last Judgment Christ will say to us, "Come, you also! Come, drunkards! Come, weaklings! Come, children of shame!" And He will say to us: "Vile beings, you are in the image of the beast and bear his mark, but come all the same, you as well!" And the wise and prudent will say, "Lord, why do You welcome them?" And He will say, "If I welcome them, you wise men, if I welcome them, you prudent men, it is because not one of them has ever been judged worthy." And He will stretch out His arms, and we will fall at His feet, and we will cry out sobbing, and then we will understand all, we will understand the Gospel of grace! Lord, Your Kingdom come!'

"The Russian is dismissed as a 'universalist'—the most abused word in the American theological vocabulary—and people go back to saving themselves. Yet the Gospel says that no matter how dutifully moral or perseveringly prayerful, we cannot save ourselves, we cannot make ourselves presentable, we cannot make ourselves lovable. To the extent that we are self-made, we let the hookers and inside-traders go first into the Kingdom. These poor people enter before us because they know they cannot save themselves, they don't thrash about trying to fix themselves, and thus are open to receive the utterly gratuitous gift of salvation.

"Paul," Daniel continued, "here is the heart of our hangup, the root of the daily dilemma of the American Christian. We fluctuate between castigating ourselves and congratulating ourselves, because we are deluded into thinking that we save ourselves. Either we develop a false sense of security from our good works and scrupulous observance of the Law, or we are appalled by our inconsistency, horrified that we haven't lived up to our lofty expectations of ourselves. The roller-coaster ride of elation and depression, self-satisfaction, and self-hatred continues. Pelagius is alive and well in the 1980s.

"Small wonder that the God we conjure in our minds bears no resemblance to the God revealed in Jesus Christ who loves us as we are and not as we should be. Our distortions and caricatures of God range from The Man Upstairs to a mean cop with a shillelagh, from a niggling customs officer rifling through our moral suitcases to a genial George Burns. Some see Him as a celestial gas, the invisible honorary president of outer space, others as a patsy God who can be manipulated by money, a Dutch Uncle God who won't rain on our parade, whose limited vocabulary does not include words like martyrdom, sacrifice, service, and self-denial.

"Paul, I know I repeat myself. But once again: We have made it too easy to be a Christian. The sole requirements are the recitation of a creed and attendance at a local church where there is no community and damn little fellowship. Christianity used to be risky business; it is no longer. Cost-free discipleship produces wimps—bland, pleasant personalities who, in Scott Peck's forceful phrase, 'belong to a church that in the name of Jesus can blasphemously co-exist with the arms race.'[8]

"Do-it-yourself religion has fostered an exaggerated form of Christian individualism, which has brought the ecumenical movement to a standstill. Jesus' cry that we all might be one as He and the Father are one goes unheeded. Despite official ecumenical committees, national and international meetings, the majority of Christians go their separate ways with near-total unconcern for the one holy catholic and apostolic Church. The formidable ecumenical gatherings, while important in their own way, present an institutional facade covering up an almost total lack of interdenominational communication on the part of ordinary Christians. Even on the local level there is little practical cooperation and scant inter-church dialogue. As George Lindbeck at Yale University has observed, 'The official facade can even be dangerous as a psychological device permitting a denomination to consider itself ecumenical, while it continues, undisturbed in its self-centered and self-satisfied groove.'

"The simple truth, Paul, is that the American Christian Church is dreadfully divided by doctrine, history, and day-to-day living. We have come a long, sad journey from the first century, when pagans exclaimed with awe and wonder, 'See how these Christians love one another!', to the twentieth century, when all over the world nonbelievers dismiss us: 'See how these Christians hate one another!' We have deprived the world of the only witness for which the Son of God asked during the supper of His love. 'Our present disunity cannot be God's will for us; it is a scandal to angels in heaven and human beings on earth.'[9]

"However, lest I paint with too broad a brush, let me say that across this country there is a congregation here, a small community there, isolated witnesses on the horizon who are crying the Gospel with their lives, conscious that they are the only copy of the New Testament many people will ever read. They see Christianity not as ritual but as a way of life. Their lives off-camera are impressive. They do things that no one can ever know about with the same sincerity as things that people can see. 'To live without risk is to risk not living' is not a cliché in their ranks. Their courageous witness in the two major moral issues of our time, war and peace, poverty and wealth, has placed them in the eye of the storm. They are splendid models for the rest of us who are so influenced by the opinion of others, who are interested in keeping a certain image in the community's eye, who desire to be liked, approved, and accepted by our peers but are not so careful about our image in God's sight—otherwise we wouldn't neglect the things that He alone sees, like personal prayer and secret acts of kindness. These little Christian bands practice a faith liberated from the clutches of the institutional church. Still, they are numerically insignificant. I have found only eight such communities in all my travels.

"As I see it, the greatest single need in the American Church is to *know* Jesus Christ, to live and breathe the words of the apostle Paul: 'All I want is to know Christ and to experience the power of His resurrection through sharing in the fellowship of His suffering.' When religion replaces such actual experience, when we lose the authority of *knowing* and rely on the authority of books, institutions, or leaders, when we let religion interpose between us and the primary experience of Jesus as the Christ, we lose the very reality religion itself describes as ultimate. Herein lies the origin of all holy wars, bigotry, intolerance, and division within the Body of Christ.

"Paul, I have spoken at great length. Pray that I may never forget that I need this teaching even more than the world does."

Paul rose to his feet. Placing his hand on Daniel's shoulder, he said, "Brother Daniel, the range and depth of your insight into the contemporary Church is remarkable. How is it that you are so knowledgeable?"

"I am a bishop. Two years ago I was appointed by the National Assembly of American Churches to freelance the country as theologian-at-large. Next month I am to report my findings and make recommendations for reform and renewal. Frankly, I am at a loss. The task is simply overwhelming."

"Daniel, is it possible for you to convene the Assembly for an emergency meeting tomorrow night? I wish to speak to them."

"You what?"

"I wish to address a prophetic word to the National Assembly."

"Who are you?"

"As I told you earlier, my name is Paul. Here are my credentials." Paul stripped off his shirt. "The brand marks on my body are those of Jesus. I am an apostle who does not owe his authority to men or his appointment to any human being. My only boast is the cross of our Lord Jesus Christ, through whom the world is crucified to me, and I to the world. I bear on my body the signature of Jesus. Can you arrange the meeting?"

"Tomorrow night at eight o'clock in the grand ballroom of the Corinthian Hotel. Paul, before you take leave, please give me your blessing."

As the sun slowly sank behind Lake Harmony, Paul knelt beside Daniel. The pair lowered their heads and remained mute and motionless for several minutes. Finally with a sigh that came straight from his heart Paul prayed: "Kneeling before the Father, this is what I pray for you, Daniel. Out of His infinite glory, may He give you the power through His Spirit for your hidden self to grow strong, so that Christ may live in your heart through faith and, then, planted in love and built on love, you will with all the saints be enabled to grasp the breadth and the length, the height and the depth, until, knowing the love of Christ, which is beyond all knowledge, you are filled with the utter fullness of God. Go in peace, my brother."

The two separated in silence.

The following night 1,500 elders gathered from every region of the country—pastors, evangelists, superintendents, bishops, cardinals, primates, archmandrakes, provincials, generals, and untitled shepherds. Some were robed and bearded, others in three-piece suits, many in clerical collars, a minority in jeans and sport shirts. The normal hospitality hour was dispensed with as a sense of hushed anticipation swept the ballroom.

Daniel mounted the platform, turned to the audience and said, "My brothers and sisters, a most extraordinary thing happened to me yesterday. I saw God in a man. There is no doubt in my mind that he is who he claims to be. I saw for myself the signature of Jesus Christ written on his body. How rich are the depths of God, how deep His wisdom and knowledge, and how impossible to penetrate His motives or understand His methods. In His limitless mercy and for His own loving purpose, God has chosen to visit His people in the United States through sending His servant Paul. My dear friends in Christ, I present to you the apostle to the nations."

The elders rose to their feet to greet Paul with applause mingled with incredulity. As the apostle reached the podium, he turned to see a 45-year-old bishop sitting in a wheelchair in the aisle beside the front row. A spinal injury suffered in an auto accident when he was thirty-three had left him paralyzed from the waist down.

Paul descended the stairwell, strode directly to the paralyzed man, and commanded, "In the name of Jesus Christ, arise and walk." The stunned bishop placed the heels of his hands on the sides of the wheelchair, hoisted himself up, and took a tentative step. Then another. And another. He pirouetted, skipped, ran, and finally danced down the center aisle. The applause was deafening as Paul returned to the podium.

"Yes, beloved of God, I am Paul, a servant of Christ Jesus who was called to be an apostle, and chosen to preach the Good News.

"Yesterday Daniel shared with me a withering appraisal of the Christian community in your country. This morning I stopped at McDonald's for an Egg McMuffin and this afternoon for a Whopper at Burger King. The 'fast food' culture of America is an apt metaphor for the spiritual state of the Church. You are overfed and undernourished on almost every level of existence: physical, emotional, intellectual, spiritual. However, this is no time for hand-wringing and breast-beating. It is clearly inappropriate to ridicule church leaders, who are only earthen vessels, for that is a grave disservice to the Body of Christ. Forget the past and press on toward what lies ahead—life on high in Christ Jesus. You are living in the 'isness' of the shall be. In this interim time, there is much to do.

"I am calling the whole Church to return to the *discipline of the secret*.[10] As you know, this ancient practice of the early Church was implemented to protect the sacred name of Jesus Christ from mockery and the mysteries of the Christian faith from profanation. Today once more the Christian enterprise, which is the building of the Kingdom of God on earth, must be a silent, hidden affair. Today the public claims of Christians have lost any claim to credibility. The words on their lips are denied by their lifestyle.

"The institutional Church, while setting out to proclaim Jesus, has often supplanted Him. 'Religion' has pushed Christ to the margin of real life, locked His Gospel in a deep freeze where inflexible dogma and unchanging law are more important than growth in Christ and breakthrough into the freedom of the sons of God. People have confused the structures of religion with both revelation and faith.

"The discipline of the secret will help the Church become liberated from itself. Disentangled from all the cultural accretions, deviations, and religious baggage of the past, the community will rediscover Christ. Only allegiance to Him and imitation of His life will make community possible and Christianity credible. Maintain a tactful silence in the presence of unbelievers. Overuse has rendered much of Christian language meaningless. When you encounter someone in grief and desolation, do not speak the biblical words known to you and available to you: Stand with him in his loneliness and brokenness, weep and mourn with him and let your silent, Spirit-filled presence be your compassion.

"The problem in Christianity today is not that something has been hidden, but that *not enough has stayed hidden*.[11] Let the Church go underground for a decade. As it lowers its profile, let it raise the ante for membership. Present to the world the image of a servant Church and preserve the mysteries of the faith, not with a showy defensive fervor but with prayer, worship, service, and a life that can only be explained in terms of God.

"In the future you will no longer be able to be a Christian without being a contemplative, and you cannot be a contemplative without having an experience of Jesus Christ. Knowledge of Jesus will guarantee the survival of faith in the secularized, politicized world of the future.

"Some would have you believe that Christianity is meant for everyone. As I did with Cephas at Antioch, I withstand them face-to-face. The Church and the Gospel lifestyle are only for small groups of committed Christians who comprise a dedicated community on the basis of their fierce loyalty to Jesus Christ. The loner is a liar; a Christian must be in community. Remember that doubting Thomas was not with the apostles when Jesus appeared in the Upper Room. Only when he returned to the community did he meet the risen Lord.

"Worship is the summit of the Church's life, the fount of all ministry, the shared solidarity that makes fidelity to Jesus possible. Worship is not for the streets, for the posters, for the media, for the masses. It is certainly not for Superdome, SilverDome, and drive-in Easter pageants. It is not for East Room exercises in American civil religion, or for Astrodome rallies. It is not bumper-sticker and slick-paper Christianity. Empowered by the risen Christ, the worshiping Church will lay down its life in martyrdom for the sake of global peace and will prove the only alternative to the nuclear night. The discipline of the secret calls each local church to be rigorous in its membership stipulations and make love of the brethren its highest priority. It will also give up its property for the sake of the needy.[12]

"I call the presbyters and leaders of the Church into daily personal fellowship with the crucified Jesus Christ, lest your proclamation of the Gospel drift into shallow platitudes and inoffensive generalities.

"I remind every follower of Jesus that discipleship means nothing less than being ready to obey Christ as unconditionally as the first disciples. Only he who believes is obedient, and only he who is obedient believes. Never confuse success in ministry or knowledge of the Bible or mastery of Christian principles and ideas with holiness and authentic discipleship. They may well be the corruption of discipleship if your life is not hidden with Christ in God.

"Banish all concern about numerical growth. As a silent leaven in the dough, be faithful to the discipline of the secret, and God who sees what is done in secret will bless you.

"My brothers and sisters in Christ, revive your drooping spirits. Place reckless confidence in the crucified One who has prevailed over every principality, power, and dominion. He has disarmed them, made a public example of them, discarded them like a garment, and led them captive in His victory procession.

"It is Paul, the apostle to the nations, wearing on his body the signature of Jesus, who speaks. May the grace and peace of the Lord Jesus Christ be with your spirit. Amen."

Dear reader, this exercise in Christian imagination may be dismissed as sheer fantasy, as the dangerous rambling of a self-styled prophet. Or perhaps it has painted accurate images of yourself, the Church, and the real world in which you live. Possibly it has altered your perspective to see a fresh landscape. The verdict of course is yours.

In this opening chapter, it is obvious that I have shared my own perception of the contemporary Church through the voice of "Daniel" and recommendations for renewal drawn from the writings of Paul. At this moment in Church history, I believe the *discipline of the secret* to be essential. The Gospel of Jesus Christ is not to be forced upon an unwilling world. To put it bluntly, people have had their bellyful of our sermonizing. They want a source of strength for their lives. We can recommend it only by making it actively present in our own. In terms of church growth for the next decade the operative principle is *Less is more*. As the Marxist leader Lenin said shortly before his death: "Give me ten men like Francis of Assisi and I will rule the world."

The following pages explore the overwhelming love of God revealed in Jesus Christ and what it means to walk the talk.

Two

The Signature
of Jesus

I know a man who for twenty-five years has steadfastly refused to allow a cross or a crucifix in his home. Far from being either superficial or shallow, he is a person of great integrity. He doesn't shout with the crowd, nor does he dismiss Christianity as a musty antique of a medieval past. Why then does he refuse? In his own words, "I can't stand the cross. It is a flat denial of all that I value in life. I am a proud man, sensual, I seek pleasure. The cross reproaches me. It says, 'You're wrong. Your life must take this shape. This is the only true interpretation of life, and life is true only when it takes this form.'" And so, he will not allow a symbol of the crucified Christ in his home. In his honesty he knows that to do so, he must commit himself to a way of life that contradicts the life he is living.

This story of one man's flight from God is nothing new.

Francis Thompson told it more than a hundred years ago in poetry when he wrote: "Down the nights and down the days; . . . I fled Him down the labyrinthine ways of my own mind; and in the midst of tears I hid from Him and under running laughter. . . ." And the Hound of Heaven replied: "Lo, all things fly thee, for thou flyest Me! Strange, piteous futile thing."

For the apostle Paul hostility to the cross is the foremost characteristic of the world. To the Galatians Paul writes that what stamps a Christian most deeply is the fact that through Jesus' cross the world is crucified to him and he to the world. To the Corinthians Paul says we manifest the life of Jesus only if we carry His death about with us. What Paul says to them applies to every Christian. We are disciples only as long as we stand in the shadow of the cross.

The Master said, "He who does not take up his cross and follow Me is not worthy of Me." Dietrich Bonhoeffer, the German Lutheran martyr, caught the true meaning of this when he wrote: "When Jesus calls a man, he bids him come and die." We have no reason or right to choose another way than the way God chose in Jesus Christ. The cross is both the symbol of our salvation and the pattern of our lives.

When our dogmatic beliefs and moral principles do not realize themselves in suffering discipleship, then our holiness is an illusion. And the world has no time for illusions. Today the Christian community does not disturb the world. Why should it? The cross is as commonplace on a pierced earring of the rock singer Madonna as it is on a tombstone.

Christian piety has trivialized the passionate God of Golgotha. Christian art has turned the unspeakable outrage of Calvary into dignified jewelry. Christian worship has sentimentalized monstrous scandal into sacred pageant. Organized religion has domesticated the crucified

Lord of glory, turned Him into a tame theological symbol. Theological symbols do not sweat blood in the night. In his landmark work *The Crucified God*, Jurgen Moltmann writes: "We have made the bitterness of the cross, the revelation of God in the cross of Jesus Christ, tolerable to ourselves by learning to understand it as a theological necessity for the process of salvation. As a result the cross loses its arbitrary and incomprehensible character."[1]

Viewed as a theological relic, the cross does not disturb our comfortable religiosity. But when the crucified risen Christ, instead of remaining an icon, comes to life and delivers us over to the fire that He came to light, He creates more havoc than all the heretics, secular humanists, and self-serving preachers put together.

There is a frightening preoccupation with trivia in the American Church today. We quibble, for heaven's sake, over the songs we sing. William Penn said, "To be like Christ is to be a Christian." And Jesus demands nothing less than the placing of our own egos and desires on the cross. Today many churches attempt to eliminate the risk and danger of this call. We cushion the risk and eliminate the danger of discipleship by drawing up a list of moral rules that give us security instead of holy insecurity. The Word of the cross, the power and wisdom of Jesus Christ crucified, is conspicuous by its absence.

Recently a friend called me long-distance to ask if I was upset by what a certain television evangelist said on his program about Roman Catholics. I replied that nothing he says upsets me; it's what he doesn't say that upsets me. Dr. Martin Marty, Lutheran professor of church history at the University of Chicago, puts it this way: "The problem is that Christianity and celebrity don't go together. A celebrity has a big ego and needs to feed it. These shows misportray government, humanism, and mainline religions. They don't convert; they confirm. I can't picture them changing people."

But changing people is the point. Weaning us from our worldly values. The apostle Paul was aware of the worldliness that had penetrated and gained ground within the Church. He said there were enemies of the cross of Christ in Galatia and Corinth, in Philippi and Rome—not so much among the waverers as among the most devout church members. Jesus did not die at the hands of muggers, rapists, or thugs. He fell into the well-scrubbed hands of ministers and lawyers, statesmen and professors—society's most respected members.

In his book *The Cost of Discipleship*, Bonhoeffer defined "cheap grace" as grace without the cross. When Jesus Christ crucified is not proclaimed and lived out in love, the Church is a bored and boring society. There is no power, no challenge, no fire—no change. We make drab what ought to be dramatic. A Christian is a lover of Christ and His cross. Ernst Kasemann says: "A man counts as a lover of the cross only insofar as it enables him to come to terms with himself and others and with the powers and enticements of the world. Under the cross, man attains manhood . . . there is no sharing in the glory of the risen Lord except in the discipleship of the cross."[2]

In April 1944, a year before his death, while imprisoned in a concentration camp in Flossenburg, Germany, Bonhoeffer wrote: "What is bothering me incessantly is the question what Christianity really is, or indeed what Christ really is for us today." That is the question each of us must spell out for himself. Who is Jesus? What does discipleship in the 1980s and 90s really involve? Everything else is a distraction. The Jesus of my journey is the crucified One. The sign of His Lordship is the cross and the cross alone. It is the signature of the risen One. The glorified Christ is identifiable with the historical Jesus of Nazareth only as the Man of the cross.

So central to the story of salvation is the signature of Jesus that Paul does not hesitate to say: "I preach only

Jesus Christ, and only about Him as crucified." When Paul arrived in Corinth, he had just returned from Athens. He was discouraged by his failure to win the Greek community through his use of natural theology. To the people of this licentious seaport town of Corinth where sexual immorality flourished, Paul abandoned the wisdom approach and preached only the folly of the cross. He proclaimed: "Jesus Christ crucified is the power of God and the wisdom of God."

In a stunning paradox, Paul tells the Corinthians: "The message of the cross is foolishness to those who are perishing, but to those being saved it is the power of God. The Jews demand signs and the Greeks demand wisdom, but we proclaim a Christ who is crucified, to the Jews a stumblingblock and to the Gentiles foolishness, but to those who are called, Christ the power of God and the wisdom of God. For the foolishness of God is wiser than men, and the weakness of God is stronger than men" (see Corinthians: 18–24).

The Greek word for foolishness suggests something that is dull, insipid—stupid not in the sense of being publicly dangerous but publicly despised, ignored because it is ridiculous. And this is precisely what Paul proclaims. His revelation runs directly counter to the expectations of Jew and Greek. The Jews looked for a Messiah; Jesus' shameful death on a cross proved to them that He wasn't the glorious liberator they awaited. The cross formed an obstacle to faith.

The Greeks were sure that the Messiah would be a philosopher greater than Plato, able to demonstrate the order and harmony of the universe. A Messiah who would challenge this cultured, intellectual piety by reversing its values and going to death on a cross, victim of the irrational and bestial in mankind, would indeed be a stupidity to the Greeks.

Yet Paul preached the Word of the cross in the power of

the Spirit, and experienced astonishing success. Jews and Greeks alike laid aside their prejudices to be swept up by the power and wisdom of the cross. For the cross is not a message about suffering but the suffering Christ "who loved me, and delivered Himself up for me" (Galatians 2:20, NAS).

If there are few power-laden, Spirit-filled Christians in the Church today, is it not because so few of us have gotten into the business of what Paul calls "dying daily" to self-centeredness in all its forms, including self-promotion and self-condemnation? A study of Church history reveals that every time the Spirit of God blows with hurricane force through the Body, it is always through those prophets and lovers who have surrendered to the folly of the cross.

Good Friday reminds us that we are not going to be helped by God's power, only by God's weakness. For power can only force us to change. Only love can move us to change. Power affects behavior, love the heart. And nothing on earth so moves the heart as suffering love. That is why the perfect expression of God's love for us is the dying figure of Jesus pleading for someone to moisten His burning lips.

In the winter of 1968–69, I lived in a cave in the mountains of the Zaragosa Desert in Spain. For seven months I saw no one, never heard the sound of a human voice. Hewn out of the face of the mountain, the cave towered 6,000 feet above sea level. Each Sunday morning a brother from the village of Farlete below dropped off food, drinking water, and kerosene at a designated spot. Within the cave a stone partition divided the chapel on the right from the living quarters on the left. A stone slab covered with potato sacks served as a bed. The other furniture was a rugged granite desk, a wooden chair, a sterno stove, and a kerosene lamp. On the wall of the chapel hung a three-foot crucifix. I awoke each morning at two A.M. and went in there for an hour of nocturnal adoration.

On the night of December 13, during what began as a long and lonely hour of prayer, I heard in faith Jesus Christ say, "For love of you I left My Father's side. I came to you who ran from Me, fled Me, who did not want to hear My name. For love of you I was covered with spit, punched, beaten, and affixed to the wood of the cross."

These words are burned on my life. Whether I am in a state of grace or disgrace, elation or depression, that night of fire quietly burns on. I looked at the crucifix for a long time, figuratively saw the blood streaming from every pore of His body and heard the cry of His wounds: "This isn't a joke. It is not a laughing matter to Me that I have loved you." The longer I looked the more I realized that no man has ever loved me and no one ever could love me as He did. I went out of the cave, stood on the precipice, and shouted into the darkness, "Jesus, are You crazy? Are You out of Your mind to have loved me so much?" I learned that night what a wise old man had told me years earlier: "Only the one who has experienced it can know what the love of Jesus Christ is. Once you have experienced it, nothing else in the world will seem more beautiful or desirable."

The Lord reveals Himself to each of us in myriad ways. For me the human face of God is the strangulating Jesus stretched against a darkening sky, vulnerable to the taunts of passersby. In another of his letters from prison, Bonhoeffer wrote, "This is the only God who counts." Christ on the cross is not a mere theological precondition for the achievement of salvation. He is God's enduring Word to the world saying, "See how much I love you. See how you must love one another."

In Robert Bolt's play *A Man for All Seasons*, Thomas More, the Chancellor of England, explains to his daughter Meg that if he took the oath of allegiance to King Henry

VIII he would betray Jesus and lose his identity. She argues that it's not his fault that the state is three-quarters bad and if he chooses to suffer for it, he is also electing himself a hero. Her father replies, "Meg, if we lived in a state where virtue was profitable, common sense would make us good, and greed would make us saintly. And we'd live like animals or angels in the happy land that needs no heroes. But since in fact we see that avarice, anger, envy, pride, sloth, lust, and stupidity commonly profit far beyond humility, chastity, fortitude, justice, and thought, and have to choose to be human at all, why then perhaps we must stand fast a little, even at the risk of being heroes."[3]

Christian love is in essence neither romantic nor heroic, writes theologian John Shea, but in a world that calls Christians who are trying to live the Sermon on the Mount naïve, irrelevant, unrealistic, simplistic, and even mad, the disciple of Jesus simply tries "to stand fast a little," vulnerable to taunts and lances.

A Polish Jew who survived the massacre of the Warsaw ghetto and later converted to Christianity discovered that on the acceptance or rejection of the Crucified hangs the meaning of discipleship: "As I looked at that man upon the Cross . . . I knew I must make up my mind once and for all, and either take my stand beside Him and share in His undefeated faith in God . . . or else fall finally into a bottomless pit of bitterness, hatred, and unutterable despair."[4]

The Christ of the New Testament is not the God of the philosophers, speaking with cool detachment about the Supreme Being. We do not expect to find the Supreme Being with spit on His face. It is jarring to discover that the invitation Jesus issues is: "Don't weep for Me; join Me. The life I have planned for you is a Christian life, much like the life I led." As Dominique Voillaune once said to me on a wintry morning in Dijon, France, "La vie est dure"—life is hard. It is hard to be a Christian, but it is too dull to be anything else. When Jesus comes into our lives with His scandalous cross in the form of mental anguish, physical suffering, and wounds of the spirit that will not close, we pray for the courage to "stand fast a little" against the insidious realism of the world, the flesh, and the devil.

The signature of Jesus: the sign of the cross. For me the most difficult and demanding dimension of discipleship on a day-in-day-out basis is the commitment to a life of unending availability. In the early stage of my journey, in the first flush of full love, the imitation of the Ebed Yahweh, God the Servant, was a romantic, even intoxicating notion. Tonight on this warm Louisiana evening, being a servant is as unsentimental as duty, as steadily demanding as need. Hurting people are always there, and sometimes the power of their need, like a suction on my spirit, drains me of everything. One of my problems with Jesus is that He always seems to come at the wrong time. Small wonder that Teresa of Avila complained: "Lord, if this is the way You treat Your friends, it's no surprise You have so few."

In words to this effect, Jesus told His listeners: "A sign indeed you will have, but it will not be the sign of the Romans being driven into the sea, or of the sun growing dark; it will be a sign of the Servant of Yahweh to be manifested first in My life and then in My death, and after that in the lives of My disciples. Their joyous commitment to the Good News of My Father's Kingdom will issue in lives of service that will permit no doubt about the validity of My message. The ultimate credentials I offer as spokesman for My heavenly Father will be the kind of lives I and My followers after Me will live."

A beautiful game plan. If indeed we lived a life in imitation of His, our witness would be irresistible. If we dared to live beyond our self-concern, if we refused to shrink from being vulnerable, if we took nothing but a compassionate attitude toward the world, if we were a counterculture to our nation's lunatic lust for pride of place, power, and possessions, if we preferred to be faithful rather than successful, the walls of indifference to Jesus Christ would crumble. A handful of us could be ignored by society, but hundreds, thousands, millions of such servants would overwhelm the world. Christians filled with the authenticity, commitment, and generosity of Jesus would be the most spectacular sign in the history of the human race. The call of Jesus is revolutionary. If we implemented it, we would change the world in a few months.

A recent issue of *Reader's Digest* featured the following five articles: "How to Stay Slim Forever," "Five Ways to Stop Feeling Tired," "How to Get Your Way," "How Safe Are the New Contraceptives?" and "What It Takes to Be Successful." A majority of Americans, the editors have apparently concluded, are fat, exhausted, frustrated, lascivious, and dissatisfied with their level of achievement. The editors may be right; if so, there is a breathtaking superficiality to our alleged interests.

The conversation of most middle-class Americans, we are told, revolves around consumption: what to buy, what was just bought, where to eat, what to eat, the price of the neighbor's house, what's on sale this week, our clothes or someone else's, the best car on the market this year, where to spend a vacation. Apparently we can't stop eating, shopping, consuming. Success is measured not in terms of love, wisdom, and maturity but by the size of one's pile of possessions.[5]

What was it Ernst Kasemann said? "A man counts as a lover of the cross only insofar as it enables him to come to terms with . . . the powers and enticements of the world." What is outrageous about the disciple of Jesus is that he can afford to be indifferent. Dead to the world but gloriously alive in Christ, he can say with Paul, "I know how to be stuffed full, and I know how to be destitute." Such an attitude is anathema to Madison Avenue. The world will perhaps respect us if we court it, and it will perhaps respect us even more if we reject it in disdain or anger; but it will hate us if we simply take no notice of its priorities or what it thinks of us. In John's Gospel the Jews are said to be incapable of believing because "they receive glory from one another." There is a radical incompatibility between human respect and faith in Jesus Christ.

It is 1:30 A.M. I go to my darkened study, turn on the overhead spotlight that shines on the crucifix, and stare at the body naked and nailed. Prostrate on the floor, I whisper "Come, Lord Jesus" over and over. I pray with the powerlessness and poverty of a child knowing that I cannot free myself; I must be set free. Simply *showing up* at the appointed time, allowing God to make the changes in me that I cannot make myself. What can happen in prayer before a symbol of the crucified Christ is described in a scene in *Man From La Mancha*.

In the play the dialogue takes place between Alonso Chiana (Don Quixote) and Aldonza, a barmaid and hooker. In his delusion, Alonso sees this tramp as an aristocrat and treats her accordingly. He calls this coarse, vulgar trollop "my lady," and again, "Dulcinea, my sweet little one." At first she is puzzled and angry. She can't understand this madman. But there is a haunting beauty about him. Why is she attracted to this mysterious man? Because out of him comes an affirmation that she is treasure and is to be prized as treasure and treated as treasure. He shatters her thick wall of defensiveness and fear.

"Dulcinea!" cries Aldonza. "My God, he knows my whole life story. I'm a slut. Yet he is calling me Dulcinea!" For this broken woman covered with shame it is a word that rises like a fiery beacon from the depths of a black sea.

Dazzling in its simplicity, transforming in its power, astounding in its wisdom, *Dulcinea* is unspeakable utterance from the mystical depths of God Himself. *Dulcinea* is stunning revelation that God reads everything differently from the way we do. You cannot miss what He is up to in His servant Don Quixote: The losers will be winners and the winners will be losers. "Believe me when I tell you that the taxgatherers and prostitutes are entering into the reign of God before you." Christianity is simpler and grander than the commentators and theologians have made it out to be: "Treat others the way you would have them treat you" is indeed the whole Law and the prophets.

Toward the end of the story, the dream world of Don Quixote is shattered and the poor old addlebrained Alonso Chiana is dying in his family's home. Aldonza breaks into his room.

Alonso does not recognize her. He is weak and sick and confused. "I don't know you," he says.

Aldonza kneels by his bedside and pleads, "Please, please say you know me."

"Is it so important?" he asks.

"Important? It is everything, everything!" she replies. "My whole life. You spoke to me and everything seemed so different."

"I spoke to you?" Alonso whispers.

"Yes, and you called me by another name, Dulcinea. When you spoke the name, an angel seemed to whisper, 'Dulcinea, Dulcinea.' "

All the pent-up longing in the human heart of Aldonza explodes as she pours out to Alonso what happened when he called her *"Dulcinea,"* the earthquake in her spirit unleashed by his love and acceptance. His calling her a "lady" awakened something in her she thought she could never be. She had been dead, frozen, immune to human emotion. The triumph of her life was not to need anyone. But he had broken into the sealed chamber of her heart and she began to unfreeze. Seeds of hope, long buried, sprang to life. She began to believe that she was *Dulcinea*. Everything was different because she had been touched by the creative love of a dreamy old man named Don Quixote.

In my study I kneel before the crucifix and see the human face of God in the strangulating Jesus stretched across a darkening sky. Throughout His passion Jesus condemned no one. Throughout His life His words were not those of blaming and shaming, accusing and condemning, threatening, bribing, and labeling. Nor should mine be. I pray this night for all television evangelists that they will preach the Word of the cross, that , in the words of my brother Billy Graham, they will be spared from excessive pride, reliance on worldly methods to sustain a budget, infatuation with success, and preoccupation with perpetuating the organization.

The Crucified One looks directly at me. His eyes are so filled with blood and tears and pain, He can hardly see me. Then from His open wounded heart, from the mystical depths of God Himself, He whispers my name. Not my given name, no more than He calls Aldonza by her given name. It is the name on the white stone (Revelation 2:17) by which He knows me. In the bright darkness of faith everything is different. I sense new life throbbing within me. The name astounds me. It signifies acceptance, affirmation, tenderness, healing, and it effects what it signifies. For His word overrides my ego-evaluation. God sees everything differently. There is peace, joy, certainty, awe, and wonder, an overwhelming sense of Mystery inexpressible. I arise knowing in the words of Paul that I am a letter from Christ written not with ink but with the Spirit of the living God, not on a stone tablet but on the fleshy tablet of my heart . . . and at least for this one day my letter will be signed with the signature of Jesus.

Prayer before a symbol of the crucified Christ prevents

religion from replacing the actual experience of the living God. Such prayer is not a luxury, for the crisis in the Church today is the gap between what we believe and what we experience.

Lord Jesus Christ, Son of God, we pray that our faith-experience of You keep pace with our creedal statements about You. Grace us with the courage to pray. Anoint us with the spirit of compassion that we may be with You in the passion of our times; that we may be poor with those who are poor, mourn with those who mourn, enter into the struggle of our generation for social justice, treat others as we would like to be treated. We pray for the courage to risk everything on You, to be with You in your faithfulness to Your mission, our mission. For this I have come into the world, to say: "Here I am, Lord, I come to do Your will."

Three

Fools
for Christ

The Church formed by the Holy Spirit on Pentecost is described in the Septuagint version of the Bible by the Greek word *ekklesia*. It is a word rich in theological content and approximates the meaning of *qahal* in the Hebrew Bible. The *qahal Yahweh* is the assembly of the Lord, a people literally called together (the root meaning of *qahal*) by God Himself. Set apart at Mount Sinai, the Jews were a covenant community, a people consecrated to the praise and worship of the one true God. They were a pilgrim people, *in the world but not of the world*, claimed as God's very own. The *qahal* of the Old Testament foreshadows the Church of the New. The *ekklesia* of Jesus Christ is the divine flowering of all that the Israel of old prepared for and pointed to. This is what Paul meant when he called the Christian community the *ekklesia*, the Lord's assembly.

But does this phrase—"A Christian is in the world but not of the world"—correspond to the reality in which we live? One of the funny things about reality is its robust resistance to theories, abstractions, and ideals. The proverb "A stitch in time saves nine" does not confront the fact of human procrastination, nor does the wisdom of Benjamin Franklin's "A penny saved is a penny earned" address the daily reality of the compulsive shopper.

To be "in the world but not of the world" implies that a Christian is not influenced, impacted, and intimidated by the values of our American culture. Isn't that an absurd proposition? Whether we like it or not, our very membership in Western society imprisons us in a set of political, economic, social, and spiritual principles that shapes our lifestyles even when we don't subscribe to it. Several years ago the front page of the *New York Times* showed a nine-year-old Vietnamese girl running toward us, her flesh aflame from napalm. A few years later papers printed the picture of a seven-year-old Libyan girl crawling toward a Red Cross shelter, both of her feet amputated by one of our "precision" bombs. We may weep at such sights, but our taxes buy the weapons that bring them about. I am compromised by the fact that one of the reasons for writing this book is to make money. I don't like that. But I am caught in and cultivated by our culture.

A critique of our culture in the light of the Gospel is imperative if the *ekklesia* of Jesus Christ is to preserve a coherent sense of itself in a world that is torn and tearing. To criticize the system of Western technological capitalism is neither unpatriotic nor un-American for as Walter Wink, professor of biblical interpretation at Auburn Theological Seminary in New York City, noted, "We cannot minister to the soul of America unless we love its soul."[1] A chastened patriotism is indispensable for the survival of the nation as well as of the Church. National attitudes and policies change only because people love their country.

I see three areas where the American Dream is counter-evangelical, in direct opposition to the message of Jesus. Our culture, as John Kavanaugh observed, "fosters and sustains a functional trinitarian god of consumerism, hedonism and nationalism. Made in the image and likeness of such a god, we are committed to lives of possessiveness, pleasure and domination."[2]

Unless the *ekklesia* of the Lord Jesus creates a countercurrent to the drift of materialism, narcissistic self-indulgence, and belligerent nationalism, Christians merely adapt to the secular environment in a tragic distortion of the Gospel. The words of Jesus are reinterpreted to mean anything, everything, and nothing. One school of thought, for example, assures us that the New Testament is filled with Oriental exaggerations, that Jesus never intended us to take the Gospel literally. What we have done is project our mechanistic Western mentality on the poetic Semitic thought patterns of Christ.

After all, no one can have a plank of wood in his eye! And what about that impossible image: "It is easier for a camel to pass through the eye of a needle than for a rich man to enter the Kingdom of God"? Such language is not only impossible but offensive. Look at the good money can do! Even Christian undertakings must be financed. And those images of the woman in labor pains found in John and the emptying of the bowels in Mark! The language is too strong. It is more prudent to render these dangerous maxims harmless. Pour as much water as possible into the fiery wine of Christ.

Such reductionisms dilute the radical demands of discipleship so that Jesus is frequently honored today for what He did not mean rather than what He did mean. An unthinking, uncritical cultural propaganda becomes more persuasive than the sayings of Jesus regarding what is real, true, good, and of enduring value.

Jesus' summons to simplicity of life, in fact, lies in diametric opposition to the consumerism of our culture. A recent article in *People* magazine quoted Charlie Sheen, star of the Oscar-winning film *Platoon,* as saying: " 'Money is energy, man.' On the downstairs sofa of his apartment are five remote control devices for various video and audio components. Upstairs is an office with computer and gym equipment. " 'I'm the definition of decadence,' he says."

An article in *Time* magazine was devoted to shopping addicts. One man explained that he had no time to waste making choices, so he bought twenty pairs of shoes at Bloomingdale's. "Possession is the whole point. I like seeing the stuff around me like a security blanket."

An issue of *Newsweek* carried a report on the formation of tomorrow's consumers: "Toymakers and animation houses now build entire kidvid shows around planned or existing lines of playthings. The programs become, in effect, little more than half-hour commercials for their toycasts."

The relentless bombardment of the media on children to buy, want, consume, prompted Thomas Merton to write: "The modern child may early in his or her existence have natural inclinations toward spirituality. The child may have imagination, originality, a simple and individual response to reality and even a tendency to moments of thoughtful silence and absorption. All these tendencies, however, are soon destroyed by the dominant culture. The child becomes a yelling, brash, false little monster, brandishing a toy gun or dressed up like some character he has seen on television. His head is filled with inane slogans, songs, noises, explosions, statistics, brand names, menaces, ribaldries and clichés. Then, when the child gets to school, he learns to verbalize, rationalize, to pace, to make faces like an advertisement, to need a car and, in short, to go through life with an empty head conforming to others, like himself, in togetherness."[3]

We Americans are programmed to be consumers. Here in New Orleans, due to the collapse of the oil and gas business, we have been in the throes of a deep recession along with the highest unemployment rate in the United States. Yet when a new multimillion-dollar shopping complex named the *Riverwalk* opened with celebrity fanfare, we were deluged with radio and TV ads, highway billboards, and flyers on our doorsteps urging us to bring our checkbooks and credit cards to the gala ribbon-cutting. Even when hard-pressed financially, we are pressured by our culture to consume. This is our identity.

Polls reveal that the making of money has become the dominant aspiration of students entering college. In a recent survey of 10,000 high school students in New Jersey, eighty-nine percent wanted to make a lot of money, eleven percent wanted positions of power. None wanted to be holy.

The insistence of Jesus on simplicity of life is un-American. Acceptance of the Gospel lifestyle would mean disaster for business. Four years ago I led a retreat for the financial community on Wall Street in New York City. For three days I observed the frenzy in the Pit (where stocks are traded) and the commodities exchange where elbowing, shoving, and aggressive jockeying for position are accepted etiquette. Though there are several prayer groups in the Wall Street area where Christian businessmen and women try to relate the Word to the Market, I left with the distinct impression that the pursuit of wealth is not esteemed so much as important, but as the supreme good in life.

Are we people of God in the world but not of the world? Or are we more capitalistic than Christian? Our culture blasphemously implies that the bottom line is really the bottom line. Church ministries are evaluated by the size of their budgets. Retirement is anxiously discussed in monetary terms. We are impressed by wealth. We go to great lengths to stand well with the moneyed and prosperous. A person's worth is measured by the dollars he or she generates. Money assumes a spiritual dimension. Stature in the community is determined by the size and geographical location of one's home, the quality of the automobile, the array of trinkets, gadgets, and creature comforts one has collected.

The prosperity gospel is but one feeble attempt to accommodate the sayings of Jesus to our consumer culture. The words of Jesus, "Do not store up treasure for yourselves on earth. . . . Do not be anxious about tomorrow. . . . You cannot be the slave of God and money," seem alien to most of us struggling to meet mortgage, car, and tuition payments. The cultural propaganda embodied in two liquor advertisements, "Living well is the best revenge" and "Sip it with arrogance," have a curious, perhaps demonic appeal. Consumerism indeed has its own spirituality.

Perhaps the darkest dimension to the accumulation of wealth is the exploitation of cheap labor to procure the luxuries we've grown used to. If you had a cup of coffee this morning as I did, you participated. If we paid the East African pickers the minimum American wage, we could not afford to drink the coffee. "In Africa a healthy young adult male cannot possibly make more than $1.50 a day picking coffee. It is no wonder that women and children are compelled to share in the picking."[4]

Let us be bold enough to ask ourselves as Christians whether the *ekklesia* of the Lord Jesus in the United States has anything to say to our nation and its ideologies of materialism, possessiveness, and the worship of financial security. Are we courageous enough to be a sign of contradiction to consumerism through our living faith in Jesus Christ? Are we committed enough to His Gospel to become a countercurrent to the drift? Or have we so accommodated the faith of our fathers to consumption that the questions of simplicity of life, sharing of resources, and radical dependence on God's providence no longer seem relevant? How do we build the Kingdom of God on earth if what we incarnate in our lives is the dogma of our culture rather than the revelation of Jesus?

The second area of American culture in opposition to the Gospel is hedonism versus purity of heart. In the March 9, 1987, issue of *People* magazine we read that the members of the rock group the Beastie Boys, by contract with Columbia Records, have "awaiting them on each stop of their current U.S. tour a protective assortment of condoms. . . . One Columbia spokesman [said], 'Two million records alleviates a lot of nervousness. It's good to be bad when it makes money.' "

At another rock concert, "hundreds of pre-teen and teen-age Madonna fans slithered out of their parents' cars in their tube skirts, bracelets dangling. . . . They are the Material Girls, the Trendies, the Madonna Wanna-Be's. . . .

"A San Antonio radio station asked young fans what they would do to meet a rock band called Motley Crue: From a thirteen-year-old girl: 'I'd do it with the Crue, till black and blue is all you see.'. . ."

A media analyst has noted that television viewers watch more incidences of intercourse between strangers than between married people.[5]

Scripture scholar John McKenzie has said: "The basis of Western civilization is the amassing of wealth through the exploitation of nature."[6] And that includes human nature. The popularity of the Beastie Boys spawns a hedonism that makes promiscuity the norm. Marketing success makes anything acceptable, even to providing condoms for one-night stands with vulnerable teenagers. The financial attractiveness of a Judith Krantz, Harold Robbins, or Jackie Collins bestseller, the awesome power of money to legitimize sexual immorality in our culture, seeds ambiguity and confusion among churchgoers as much as anywhere else. Last year the divorce rate in the American Christian community was one percent above the national average.

I am told, and I am sure you have been told, that I'm

living in the Stone Age if I suggest that promiscuity or marital infidelity is unacceptable in the life of a disciple of Jesus Christ. Should you proclaim with Paul that the body is for the Lord and the Lord for the body, that you are not your own property, that you have been bought and paid for with the blood of Christ, that your body is a temple of the Holy Spirit, you will be subjected to mockery and derision. "At our annual shareholders meeting in Las Vegas each year," a businessman told me, "the sexual behavior of Christians is no different from that of unbelievers. And why not? Everybody has a good time and nobody gets hurt."

The third area of American culture in conflict with the Gospel is domination through violence versus obedience to the Word. As we said earlier, only he who believes is obedient, and only he who is obedient believes. In His inaugural address, the Sermon on the Mount, Jesus declared: "Blessed are the peacemakers; they shall be called children of God." The question of peace in a violent world is so important that I do not believe anyone who takes the Christian faith seriously can afford to neglect it. I am not suggesting that you have to swim out to a Polaris submarine with a banner between your teeth, but it is absolutely necessary to take a serious and articulate stand on the issue of nuclear war. And I mean *against* nuclear war. The passivity, the apparent indifference of many Christians on the issue, and worse still the active belligerency of some religious spokesmen, is rapidly becoming one of the most frightful scandals in the history of Christendom. The *ekklesia* must proclaim that Western civilization "will escape the ultimate horror only by attending to the person and the words of Jesus Christ. Like Paul, that is all we have to say; so for Christ's sake let us say it."[7]

In the Business section of *USA Today*, the newspaper with the second largest circulation in the United States, we find: " 'The character of Rambo is a great identity character for young American males,' said the vice president of American Multi Cinema. . . . 'It's got the violence, the revenge, the one guy against the world appeal,' says Cinemascope President Edward Mintz. 'I see it as a healthy antidote to all the peace-love junk of the '60s,' says Art Murphy, an industry analyst for *Variety* magazine."

An Associated Press note: Clint Eastwood, the tough guy actor who gave President Reagan one of his best lines—"Make my day"—is the Number One hero of America's 18- to 24-year-olds, a poll showed.

"Syndicated columnist Jeffrey Hart suggested that the president give a speech with this ending paragraph: 'In the future, and on principle, we guarantee that we will retaliate for the death or injury of a U.S. citizen at the ratio of 500 to 1. As I speak to you, I have received word that 15 Shiite villages and their inhabitants no longer exist.' "[8]

Jeffrey Hart is a Christian. I find this profoundly disturbing. We are a nation calling itself a believing people, but which lives in direct disobedience to the will of God. It is this vengeful spirit of retaliation, so contrary to the Gospel, that reminds me of Mark Twain's famous War Prayer in which he skewered the hypocrisy of Christians:

> O Lord our Father, our young patriots, idols of our hearts, go forth to battle—be Thou near them! With them, in spirit, we also go forth from the sweet peace of our beloved firesides to smite the foe! Lord our God, help us to tear their soldiers to bloody shreds with our shells; help us to cover their smiling fields with the pale forms of their patriot dead; help us to drown the thunder of the guns with the shrieks of their wounded, writhing in pain; help us to lay waste their humble homes with a hurricane of fire; help us to wring the hearts of their unoffending widows [and leave them and] their little children to wander unfriended the wastes of their desolated land in rags and hunger and thirst, sports of the sun flames of summer and the icy winds of winter, broken in spirit, worn with travail,

imploring Thee for the refuge of the grave and denied it—
for our sakes who adore Thee, Lord, blast their hopes,
blight their lives, protract their bitter pilgrimage, make
heavy their steps, water their way with tears, stain the
white snow with the blood of their wounded feet! We ask
it, in the spirit of Love, of Him who is the Source of Love,
and Who is the ever-faithful refuge and friend of all that
are sore beset and seek His aid with humble and contrite
hearts. Amen.[9]

As in Twain's day we continue to confuse nationalized
faith with fidelity to Jesus Christ. Jingoism and Christianity become synonymous in the belief that God is pleased
with, beholden to, partial to, and identified with our land.
Such was the rationale behind the atomic destruction of
Hiroshima and Nagasaki that vaporized a couple of hundred thousand civilian non-combatants in order to "save
American lives."

"The willingness of the majority of believers to accept
the nuclear bomb, with all that it implies, with no more
than a shadow of theoretical protest, is almost unbelievable, and yet it has become so commonplace that no one
wonders at it anymore."[10] The pragmatic wisdom of
"self-defense" and "national security" masks our childish
fantasies of revenge, where we can devastate the enemy in
such a way that there is no possibility of retaliation. Our
Clint Eastwoods, our Charles Bronsons, our subway vig-
ilantes populate our dreams, our prayers, and our illusions. A Christian is in the world but not of the world?

Ernest Becker, in his book *Escape from Evil*, has remarked
that one way we escape from evil is to project it on others.
So we become a fierce nation toppling foreign govern-
ments at will for "good and noble" reasons. The method
for establishing domination is not reverence but violence.
"And although we give lipservice to Jesus, we give every
other kind of service to Caesar and Mars [the god of
war]."[11]

The spirit of domination through force is irreconcilable with obedience to the Gospel of Jesus Christ. Christians have only one Master. Following Him is incompatible with any state of servitude to any other. Jesus couched His teachings in language that any twelve-year-old can understand. He said unequivocally, blessed are those who make peace, not war. The issue of the production, possession, and use of nuclear weapons must be discussed in terms of our Christian identity, not in terms of national security, the Russian threat, or safeguarding our standard of living. The arms race is not a political football but a deeply spiritual matter. Mass murder in the name of democracy or patriotism is the idolatry of the nation-state. The prophetic task and pastoral obligation of the *ekklesia* of Jesus Christ—a people called together, set apart, and consecrated to the worship of God—is to proclaim God's peace and love in the actual situation of our broken and tormented world.

Calling peacemakers "bleeding hearts, do-gooders, and good samaritans" with a tone of condescension indicates an unacknowledged alienation from the Gospel. When will Christians be honest enough to admit that they don't believe in Jesus Christ? That the Nazarene carpenter must be dismissed as a romantic visionary, a starry-eyed reformer hopelessly out of touch with the "real" world of domination, aggression, and power? Only when they realize that they have embraced their culture as their false god!

If Christian men and women are to live the Gospel today in our post-industrial American culture, if we are to be in the world and not of the world, then we must be willing to assume personal responsibility for the ways in which our faith has been accommodated to consumerism, hedonism, and nationalism—to possessiveness, pleasure, and domination. And we must be willing to repent, reform, and be renewed.

The *ekklesia* is the living extension of Jesus Christ in time and space. It is a countercurrent to the drift into cultural idolatry. The Church in American society today is, of necessity, a community of resistance to the gods of modern life—nuclear stockpiling, the nation, money, ego, sexual muscle, racism, pride of place. We are the pilgrim people of God with no lasting city here on earth, a community of free men and women whose freedom is not limited by the frontiers of a world that is itself in chains.

Albert Camus once said: "The only way to deal with an unfree world is to become so absolutely free that your very act of existence is an act of rebellion." There is nothing more maddening to the world than a free man or woman in Christ Jesus. People must not look to the *ekklesia* to reinforce the values of their culture, or to dust off on Sunday morning the idols they have been living by during the week.

The early Church was built on small groups of people who came together to support one another in a whole new way of life. These primitive communities were visible evidence of a real alternative to the status quo of their culture. Today we desperately need small bands of people who take the Gospel at face value, who realize what God is doing in our time, and who are living proof of being in the world but not of the world. These "base" communities or neighborhood churches should be small enough for intimacy, kindred enough for acceptance, and gentle enough for criticism. Gathered in the name of Jesus, the community empowers us to incarnate in our lives what we believe in our hearts and proclaim with our lips.

Of course, we must not romanticize such groups. It is all too easy to envision a cozy, harmonious little fellowship where everyone is tuned in on the same wavelength, to love the dream of community more than the sin-scarred members who comprise it, to fantasize heroic deeds for the Lord, and to hear the applause in heaven and on earth as we shape an angelic *koinonia*.

The reality is otherwise. Egos collide, personalities

conflict, power-brokers intrude, anger and resentment surface, risk is inevitable. "It is less like utopia than a crucible or refiner's fire."[12] My own experience here in New Orleans bears witness to that. In struggling to move from pseudocommunity (conformity to an imagined norm) to authentic community (where differences are celebrated and mutual acceptance prevails), our base group of thirteen has discovered that we do not think ourselves into a new way of living but live our way into a new kind of thinking.

The experience of community is neither a luxury for the spiritually affluent nor a panacea for the lonely, bored, and idle. It is a necessity for every Christian. It is my personal conviction that this is what Jesus meant for His Church and what Paul means when he speaks of the *ekklesia*—small Christian communities praying and worshiping together, healing, forgiving, reconciling, supporting, challenging, and encouraging one another. Peck says: "There can be no vulnerability without risk; there can be no community without vulnerability; there can be no peace—and ultimately no life—without community."[13]

We need a group of people around us who support and understand us, the base community. Even Jesus needed this: He called them "The Twelve," the first Christian community. We need perspective on the present so we pray together, we need accountability so we share our lives with each other, we need a vision of the future so we dream together.

And our dreams are not mere wishful thinking; rather they are charged with hope and promise because the crucified, risen Jesus has prevailed over every principality, power, and dominion. He has unmasked their illusions, exposed their lies, shown them for what they are. The risen Christ stands free from their threats and control. In union with Him we conquer consumerism, hedonism, and nationalism by the power of God's love. We confront the world's powers—political tyranny, economic oppression, the nuclear meltdown—not merely with our own strength, resources, and resistance, but with the very life of the risen Christ, knowing that things impossible with men are possible with God.

Naturally the countercultural lifestyle—simplicity of life, purity of heart, and obedience to the Gospel—will take us to the same place that it took Jesus: the cross. All roads lead to Calvary for we preach "Jesus Christ crucified—a stumblingblock to Jews, an absurdity to Gentiles; but to those who are called, Jews and Gentiles alike, Christ the power of God and the wisdom of God."

Simplicity, purity, and obedience to the Word will leave us weak and powerless in the world's eyes because we can no longer call upon our possessions and privileged positions as security. We will be subject to derision and outrage because authentic discipleship is a life of sublime madness. Injury and insult are promised to those who labor for the sake of righteousness. Paul's word to the Galatians is utter folly to our American culture: "God forbid that I should glory, save in the cross of our Lord Jesus Christ, by whom the world is crucified unto me, and I unto the world" (Galatians 6:14, KJV).

A Christian living in the world but not of the world is a sign of contradiction to the compromises that many within the Church have settled for. The disciple of Jesus will be made to look and feel like a fool. Yet, fools for Christ formed the early Church. And as that tiny band of believers grew, the world witnessed the power in such foolishness.

"That same foolishness is the only hope we have of breaking free. The greatest threat to any system is the existence of fools who do not believe in the ultimate reality of that system. To repent and believe in a new reality— that is the essence of conversion."[14] We join the *ekklesia* whose purpose is to make visible this new reality in the world.

In order to live this radical lifestyle, Christians must

become Christians. True disciples see Christianity as a way of life on and off camera. Obviously, it will not appeal to everyone. The ranks of church membership will be thinned. Christians will look different and act different from other people because they are different. The name of Jesus will no longer be casually mouthed or the Christian mysteries profaned. The scandals that have recently rocked the Body of Christ will be seen in perspective as a "purifying dawn" heralding the daylight of lived faith in the living God.

Easter morning vindicated the way of Jesus and validated the authority of His Lordship. The Master told us never to underestimate the power of our culture. Our world, full of incredible foolishness, will insist that we are the fools. Yet Easter convinces us of God's wisdom and His power to transform our world. Our faith in the risen Jesus is the power that overcomes ourselves, our culture, and our world.

In the words of Paul in Romans 12: "Do not conform any longer to the pattern of this world, but be transformed by the renewing of your mind. Then you will be able to test and approve what God's will is—his good, pleasing and perfect will" (verse 2, NIV).

4

Discipleship Today

In January '87 the postman delivered an invitation from the United States Senate and House of Representatives to attend the National Prayer Breakfast in the Washington Hilton with the President and Mrs. Reagan and other government leaders. I was asked to speak at two dinners on the night preceding the breakfast and at two seminars the following morning.

My wife, Roslyn, read the invitation and remarked, "Brennan, I knew you when you were nothin'." Simone, eighteen, and Nicole, sixteen, were heading out the door to school. Simone said, "You're still nothin'." And Nicole added, "You'll never amount to nothin'." A Russian *staretz* once said, "If you pray for humility, be careful. Humility is learned through humiliations."

What caught my eye on the invitation was a quote from

Francis of Assisi. In "Letter to Rulers of People," he wrote: "Keep a clear eye toward life's end. Do not forget your purpose and destiny as God's creature. What you are in his sight is what you are and nothing more. Remember that when you leave this earth, you can take with you nothing that you have received—fading symbols of honor, trappings of power—but only what you have given: a full heart enriched by honest service, love, sacrifice and courage."

For Francis discipleship or the following of Christ was not simply the most important thing in life; it was the only thing in life. It was literally a matter of eternal life and death. "I am what I am in God's sight and nothing more." Discipleship demands that we put aside all nonessentials, stop playing word games, and come to the essence of things.

The essence for the follower of Jesus lies in living by faith and not by religion. Living faith consists in constantly redefining and reaffirming our identity with Jesus, measuring ourselves against Him—not measuring Him against our church dogmas and local heroes. Jesus is the light of the world. In His light we see that many of the burning theological issues in the Church today are neither burning nor theological; in an era of evangelical nationalism, we discover that it is not mere rhetoric that Jesus demands but personal renewal, fidelity to the Word, and creative conduct. As Emile Leger said when he left his mansion in Montreal to go live in a leper colony in Africa, "The time for talking is over."

Discipleship means living one day at a time as though Jesus were near, near in time, near in place, the witness of our motives, our speech, our behavior. As indeed He is.

Religiosity per se is not discipleship; in fact, it may be a safe refuge from the revolutionary lifestyle proposed by Jesus. In October 1917, the Russian Revolution was launched and human history was given a new dimension.

"The story goes that that very month the Russian Orthodox Church was assembled in Council. A passionate
debate was in progress about the color of the surplice to be
used in liturgical functions. Some insisted vehemently
that it had to be white. Others, with equal vehemence,
that it had to be purple. Nero fiddled while Rome burnt."[1]
Coming to grips with a Revolution, Anthony DeMello
comments, is infinitely more bothersome than organizing
a beautiful liturgy. I'd rather say my prayers than get
involved in neighborhood quarrels.

On New Year's Eve, a sincere Christian may decide the
time has come to live like a disciple, so he or she resolves
the following: I am going to get into the Word every day,
join a prayer group, find a spiritual guide, do more
spiritual reading, go to church more often, increase my
devotional time, experiment with fasting, and shout,
"Praise the Lord" upon awakening and retiring. Many
disciples do these things, yet do not follow Jesus. Though
unmistakably religious, they have never been converted.

What is the relationship between discipleship and religious practices? The latter sustain the Christian life. It is
impossible to keep Christian values in focus if we do not
read Scripture and pray and lean on others for support
and direction. Our culture, which panders to appetite,
curiosity, and distraction, and the media, which scratches
the itch for possessions, will otherwise prove too strong
for us.

"We need reminders, symbols, stories, exhortations,
living models, times out for reflection and celebration.
These things are indispensable supports. The error is to
think these things *are* the Christian life. Just as Jesus'
practice of prayer was in the service of a whole way of life,
a means rather than an end, so must ours be. Insofar as
prayer, reading, sacraments and spiritual direction support genuine Christian living, that is, Christian attitudes,
relationships, choices and actions, they are useful. When

they become an escape from the more difficult demands of Christian living, they are the corruption of discipleship. The question at the Last Judgment is not 'How religious was your talk?' nor 'How much time did you spend in prayer?' nor 'Was your faith orthodox in every respect?' but 'How did you respond to needy brothers and sisters?' This is the one reliable measure of discipleship."[2]

In preparing this book, I contacted several Christian communities throughout the United States seeking their understanding of discipleship. The answers were varied, illuminating, and often profound. Combining their insights with my own (and aware of my personal preferences, prejudices, and partial grasp of truth), I shall focus on three features of Jesus' life and teaching and their immediate importance for discipleship today.

Jesus lived for God. The central theme in the personal life of Jesus of Nazareth was His growing intimacy with, trust in, and love for His Father. His inner life was centered totally on God. For Him the Father meant everything. "Father, glorify Your Son that Your Son might glorify You." The will of the Father was the air that He breathed. *"I* do nothing on My own, but only what I see the Father doing." The Father's will was a river of life, a bloodstream from which He drew life more profoundly than from His mother. "Whoever does the will of My Father is My mother, My brother, and My sister." He lived secure in His Father's acceptance. "As the Father has loved Me, so have I loved you." Christ's total orientation was to His Father.

Living for God finds its foremost expression in prayer. The heart of discipleship lies in commitment and worship, not reflection and theory. The Spirit of Jesus provides a way for us to live on the surface and out of the depths at the same time. On the surface level, we can think, dialogue, plan, and be fully present to the demands of the daily routine. Simultaneously and deep within, we can be in prayer, adoration, thanksgiving, and attentiveness to the Spirit. The secret places of the heart become a sanctuary of praise in the noisy playpen of the marketplace. What masters of the interior life recommend is the discipline of "centering down" throughout the day: a quiet, persistent turning to God while driving, cooking, conversing, writing, and so on. After weeks and months of practice, relapses, discouragement, and returns to the Center, this discipline becomes a habit. Brother Lawrence called it *The Practice of the Presence of God*.

Herein lies the secret, I believe, of the inner life of Jesus of Nazareth. Christ's communion with Abba in the inner sanctuary of His soul transformed His vision of reality, enabling Him to perceive God's love and care behind the complexities of life. Practicing the presence helps us to discern the providence of God at work especially in those dark hours when the signature of Jesus is being traced in our flesh. (You may wish to try it right now. Lower the book, center down, and offer yourself to the indwelling God).

"If anyone loves me, he will obey my teaching. My Father will love him, and we will come to him and make our home with him"(John 14:23, NIV). In muffled cries of praise, a disciple turns humbly to this indwelling God throughout the day. He is alert to the outer world of sound, sense, and meaning: This is not a discipline in absentmindedness. He walks and talks, works and plays, laughs and cries in full presence to tasks and persons. Behind the scenes, the rhythm of prayer and interior worship continues. A cry of thanksgiving is his last word before falling asleep and his first upon awakening.

The frequent repetition of the name *Jesus* or *Abba, Father* throughout the day will prove helpful. Even a mechanical recitation of the name will suffice; eventually it gets into your subconscious and a real transformation of mind and heart takes place.

The early days of this discipline are awkward, painful, and rewarding. Awkward because it requires vigilance and discipline. Painful because the lapses and relapses are frequent. (When we slip and forget God's presence within, it is self-defeating to spend time in regrets and self-condemnation. We begin anew right where we are, offer this broken worship to Jesus Christ, and thank Him for the grace to center down once again.) Finally, it is rewarding because life lived in the inner sanctuary is the abundant life that Jesus promised.

Philosopher William James said: "In some people religion exists as a dull habit, in others as an acute fever." Jesus did not endure the shame of the cross to hand on a dull habit. (If you don't have the fever, dear reader, a passion for God and His Christ, drop this book, fall on your knees, and beg for it; turn to the God you half-believe in and cry out for His baptism of fire.)

The fifteenth-century mystic Meister Eckhart wrote: "There are plenty of Christians to follow the Lord halfway, but not the other half. They will give up possessions, friends and honors, but it touches them too closely to disown themselves." Eckhart's words touch the nerve of this chapter on discipleship. I am not speaking of multiplying altars and sacrifices or plunging into a series of spiritual activities; or lengthening the time of formal prayer or getting involved in more church-related organizations. I am not speaking of fasts, rituals, devotions, liturgies, or prayer meetings. I am speaking of a life lived completely for God, the astonishing life of a committed disciple who is willing to follow Jesus the other half; a life of surrender without reservations. I propose it in humility and boldness. I mean this literally, utterly, completely; I mean it for you and me.

To be like Christ is to be a Christian.

There is a revolutionary explosiveness to this proposal. When a disciple lives his or her life wholly and entirely for

God, stands ready to go the other half, to walk hand-in-hand with the Jesus for whom God is everything, the limitless power of the Holy Spirit is unleashed. God breaks through, miracles occur, the world is renewed, and history is changed. Disciples the world over, living in the light who is Christ, know with utter clarity that abortion and nuclear weapons are but two sides of the same hot coin minted in hell, that Christians stand upright beside the Prince of Peace and refuse to fall prostrate before the shrine of national security, that we are a life-giving and not a death-dealing people of God, that we live under the sign of the cross and not the sign of the bomb. In the next decade, there is nothing more important than to see the human race endowed with prophets and lovers, a community of authentic disciples who, like the One they follow, live wholly and entirely for God.

To this extraordinary life of discipleship, Jesus calls us—not as a lovely ideal, not as a quaint, peculiar, and charming lifestyle to aim at, but as a serious, concrete, and realistic program of life to be lived here and now by you and me.

"This is something radically different from the mild, conventional religion which, with respectable skirts held back by dirty fingers, tries to fish the world out of the sinkhole of its own selfishness. Our churches are full of such amiable and respectable people. We have plenty of Christians to follow Jesus the first half of the way. Many of us have become as halfheartedly and conventionally religious as were the church folk of two thousand years ago, against whose mildness, mediocrity and passionlessness Jesus Christ and His disciples flung themselves with all the passion of a glorious new discovery and with all the energy of builders of the Kingdom of God on earth."[3]

A life lived for God is remarkably well-rounded. Its joys are genuine, its peace profound, its humility deep, its power formidable, its love enveloping, its simplicity that of a trusting child. It is the life and power in which the prophets and apostles moved. It is the life and power of Jesus of Nazareth who taught that "when the eye is single, the whole body is full of light." It is the life and power of the apostle Paul who resolved not to know anything save Jesus Christ and Him crucified. It is the life and power of Francis of Assisi who relived the Gospel more closely than any person since apostolic times. It is the life and power of countless unknown saints throughout the ages. It is the life and power of many readers of this book who nod with recognition as they read. It is the life and power that can break forth in our tottering Western culture, renew the Body of Christ, and build the new heavens and the new earth.

To those disciples wishing to live their lives wholly for God, I recommend praying the Lord's Prayer three times each day—in the morning, at noon, and in the evening. This recommendation may sound too simplistic for a generation working so hard at prayer, groping in the dark for its mystic edges.

We have never entirely given up our efforts to improve on the way Jesus told us to pray. We have made prayers fancier, longer, and sometimes more dramatic, but we have never made them as deep as the Lord's Prayer. Where in days past people fasted and kept vigil in hopes of trapping the Holy Spirit, we now hold symposiums, workshops, and seminars on prayer in the same quest. We have never finished the search for something more than the staples of life that Jesus underscores in the prayer to the Father.

The devout Jew prayed the Shema three times daily. This prayer, found in Deuteronomy 6:4–5, reads: "Listen, Israel: Yahweh our God is the one Yahweh. You shall love Yahweh your God with all your heart, with all your soul, with all your strength" (JB). This prayer was the badge of the Jews, the sign of belonging to God's chosen people. It

72

consecrated them to the service of Yahweh and failure to pray it separated them from the Covenant. The Jews gloried in the fact that God had revealed His name as Yahweh to them alone.

Christians glory in the truth that Jesus has revealed to them alone the name of God as "Abba." The Lord's Prayer is the Christian Shema. Three times daily, it is a joyful renewal of our baptism into Christ Jesus and our initiation into the *ekklesia*. An ancient Christian document, the Didache, dating back to the second century, advises: "Do not pray like the Pharisees. You must pray this way three times a day: Our Father. . . ."

Godfrey Diekmann recommends that each time we pray the Lord's Prayer we pay special attention to the petition "Forgive us our trespasses as we forgive those who trespass against us." Diekmann says, "The pagans marvelled at the early Christian community saying, 'See how they love one another!' Is it possible that the Lord's Prayer prayed three times a day deliberately, conscious of its basic implication, was a major formative factor in gaining that reputation for the early Christians?"

The second major feature of Jesus' life: *Jesus lived for others*. He was not simply called but actually was "the friend of publicans and sinners." He befriended the rabble, the riffraff of His own culture. "One of the mysteries of the gospel tradition is this strange attraction of Jesus to the unattractive, his strange desire for the undesirable, his strange love for the unlovely. The key to this mystery is, of course, the Father. Jesus does what he sees the Father doing, he loves those whom the Father loves."[4]

The gentleness of Jesus with sinners flowed from His ability to read their hearts and to detect the sincerity and goodness there. Behind men's grumpiest poses and most puzzling defense mechanisms, behind their arrogance and airs, behind their silence, sneers, and curses, Jesus saw little children who hadn't been loved enough and who had ceased growing because someone had ceased believing in them. His extraordinary sensitivity and compassion caused Jesus (and later the apostles) to speak of the faithful as children no matter how tall, rich, clever, and successful they might be.

When Jesus tied a towel 'round His waist, poured water into a copper basin, and washed the feet of the apostles (the dress and duty were those of a slave), the Maundy Thursday revolution began, and a whole new idea of greatness in the Kingdom of God emerged. Jesus is Servant, ministering to the needs of others. "If I then, the Lord and Master, have washed your feet, you should wash each other's feet. I have given you an example so that you may copy what I have done to you" (John 13:14–15, JB).

What a shocking reversal of our culture's priorities and values. To prefer to be the servant rather than the lord of the household, to merrily taunt the gods of power, prestige, honor, and recognition, to refuse to take oneself seriously, to live without gloom by a lackey's agenda, these are the attitudes and actions that bear the stamp of authentic discipleship. In effect, Jesus said: Blessed are you if you love to be unknown and regarded as nothing. All things being equal, to prefer contempt to honor, to prefer ridicule to praise, to prefer humiliation to glory—those are formulas of greatness in the new Israel of God.

So central is Jesus' teaching on humble apprenticeship and serving love as the essence of discipleship, that at the Last Judgment, Christ Himself disappears and is recognizable only in our brothers and sisters: "What you did to those around you, you did to Me" (see Matthew 25:40). In this context, the words of Mother Teresa are impressive. At the dedication of a hospice for the terminally ill in New York City, she said, "Each AIDS victim is Jesus in a distressing disguise."

Jesus' ministry of service is rooted in His compassion for

the lost, lonely, and broken. Why does He love losers, failures, those on the margin of social respectability? Because the Father does. "He who sees Me, sees the Father."

Charlie Brown says, "I love humanity. It's people I can't stand." In Jesus' life and teaching, it is the flesh-and-blood person, not the generality, who is to be treated with compassion: the person there in front of me, not the abstraction.

Dominique Voillaume has impacted my life as few people ever have. One New Year's morning in Saint-Remy, France, seven of us in the community of the Little Brothers of Jesus were seated at a table in an old stone house. We were living an uncloistered contemplative life among the poor with the days devoted to manual labor and the nights wrapped in silence and prayer.

The breakfast table talk grew animated when our discussion turned to our daily employment. The German brother remarked that our wages were substandard (60¢ per hour). I commented that our employers were never seen in the parish church on Sunday morning. The French brother suggested that this showed hypocrisy. The Spanish brother said they were rude and greedy. The tone grew more caustic, and the salvos got heavier. We concluded that our avaricious bosses were nasty, self-centered cretins who slept all day Sunday and never once lifted their minds and hearts in thanksgiving to God.

Dominique sat at the end of the table. Throughout our harangue he never opened his mouth. I glanced down the table and saw tears rolling down his cheeks. "What's the matter, Dominique?" I asked. His voice was barely audible. All he said was, "Ils ne comprennent pas." *They don't understand!* How many times since that New Year's morning has that single sentence of his turned resentment of mine into compassion. How often have I reread the passion story of Jesus in the Gospels through the eyes of

Dominique Voillaume, seen Jesus in the throes of His death agony, beaten and bullied, scourged and spat upon, saying, "Father, forgive them, *ils ne comprennent pas.*"

The following year, Dominique, a lean, muscular six-foot-two, always wearing a navy blue beret, learned at age 54 that he was dying of inoperable cancer. With the community's permission he moved to a poor neighborhood in Paris and took a job as night watchman at a factory. Returning home every morning at eight A.M. he would go directly to a little park across the street from where he lived and sit down on a wooden bench. Hanging around the park were marginal people, drifters, winos, "has-beens," dirty old men who ogled the girls passing by.

Dominique never criticized, scolded, or reprimanded them. He laughed, told stories, shared his candy, accepted them just as they were. From living so long out of the inner sanctuary, he gave off a peace, a serene sense of self-possession and a hospitality of heart that caused cynical young men and defeated old men to gravitate toward him like bacon toward eggs. His simple witness lay in accepting others as they were without questions and allowing them to make themselves at home in his heart. Dominique was the most nonjudgmental person I have ever known. He loved with the heart of Jesus Christ.

One day, when the ragtag group of rejects asked him to talk about himself, Dominique gave them a thumbnail description of his life. Then he told them with quiet conviction that God loved them tenderly and stubbornly, that Jesus had come for rejects and outcasts just like themselves. His witness was credible because the Word was enfleshed on his bones. Later one old-timer said, "The dirty jokes, vulgar language, and leering at girls just stopped." One morning Dominique failed to appear on his park bench. The men grew concerned. A few hours later, he was found dead on the floor of his cold-water flat. He died in the utter obscurity of a Parisian slum.

Dominique Voillaume never tried to impress anybody, never wondered if his life was useful or his witness meaningful. He never felt he had to do something great for God. He did keep a journal. It was found shortly after his death in the drawer of the nightstand, by his bed. His last entry is one of the most astonishing things I have ever read: "All that is not the love of God has no meaning for me. I can truthfully say that I have no interest in anything but the love of God which is in Christ Jesus. If God wants it to, my life will be useful through my word and witness. If He wants it to, my life will bear fruit through my prayers and sacrifices. But the usefulness of my life is His concern, not mine. It would be indecent of me to worry about that."

In this Little Brother of Jesus, Dominique Voillaume, I saw the reality of a life lived entirely for God and for others. After an all-night prayer vigil, he was buried in an unadorned pine box in the backyard of the Little Brothers' house in Saint-Remy. A simple wooden cross over the grave with the inscription "Dominique Voillaume, a witness to Jesus Christ" said it all. More than 7,000 people gathered from all over Europe to attend the funeral. He was a splendid practitioner of the *discipline of the secret.*

Any spirituality that does not lead from a self-centered to an other-centered mode of existence is bankrupt. For many of us the journey out of preoccupation with self begins with self-acceptance. In order to live for others I must be able to live with myself. Years ago the Swiss psychologist Carl Jung asked: What if I should discover that the least of the brothers of Jesus, the one crying out most desperately for reconciliation, forgiveness, and acceptance, is myself? That I myself stand in need of the alms of my own kindness, that I myself am the enemy who must be loved, what then? Will I do for myself what I do for others?

My own need for self-acceptance singed my conscience in the terminal of the Kansas City airport. I was en route from Clearwater, Florida, to Des Moines, Iowa, to lead a retreat. Bad weather rerouted my plane to Kansas City where we had a half-hour layover. I was wandering around the terminal in my clerical collar, when a man approached me and asked if he could make his confession. We sat down in the relative privacy of the Delta Crown Room and he began: "Bless me, Father, for I have sinned. I am a priest and have not been to confession for twelve years. . . ." His life had been scarred with serious sin. Midway through, he started to cry. Embracing him I found myself in tears reassuring him of the joy in the Kingdom over the return of a repentant sinner and reminding him that the Prodigal Son experienced an intimacy with his father that his sinless, self-righteous brother never knew.

The priest's face was transfigured. The merciful love of the redeeming God broke through his guilt and self-hatred. I prayed a prayer of thanksgiving for the Lord's unbearable forgiveness, infinite patience, and tender love, and extended the absolution of Jesus Christ. The priest wept for joy. As we parted, he glowed with the radiance of a saved sinner.

As I fastened my seatbelt in the DC-10, I heard an inner voice like a bell sounding deep in my soul: *Brennan, would you do for yourself what you have just done for your brother? Would you so eagerly and enthusiastically forgive yourself, accept yourself, and love yourself?* Then words that I had heard Francis MacNutt speak seven years earlier at a gathering in Atlantic City, New Jersey, pierced my heart: "If the Lord Jesus Christ has washed you in His own blood and forgiven you all your sins, how dare you refuse to forgive yourself?"

Self-hatred is an indecent luxury that no disciple can afford. Self-hatred subtly reestablishes me as the center of my focus and concern. Biblically that is idolatry. Gentleness toward myself issues in gentleness with others. It is also the precondition for my approach to God in prayer. Small wonder that the late Paul Tillich defined faith as "the courage to accept acceptance."

A life of love lived unpretentiously for others flowing out of a life lived for God *is* the imitation of Christ and the only authentic discipleship. A life of service through the unglamorous, unpublicized works of mercy is the core of the *discipline of the secret* and the most effective means of evangelization. In his book *The Scent of Love* Keith Miller puts it this way:

The early Church grew "not because of the charisms of Christians—such as the gift of speaking in tongues—and not because Christianity was such a palatable doctrine (to the contrary, it is about the most unpalatable doctrine there is) but because they had discovered the secret of community. Generally they did not have to lift a finger to evangelize. Someone would be walking down a back alley in Corinth or Ephesus and would see a group of people sitting together talking about the strangest things—something about a man and a tree and an execution and an empty tomb. What they were talking about made no sense to the onlooker. But there was something about the way they spoke to one another, about the way they looked at one another, about the way they cried together, the way they laughed together, the way they touched one another that was strangely appealing. It gave off the scent of love. The onlooker would start to drift farther down the alley, only to be pulled back to this little group like a bee to a flower. He would listen some more, still not understanding, and start to drift away again. But again he would be pulled back, thinking, I don't have the slightest idea what these people are talking about, but whatever it is, I want part of it."[5]

The third feature of Jesus' life and teaching crucial for discipleship in the world today is *simplicity of life*. When Jesus tells us not to lay up treasure for ourselves on earth, it is because He knows that where our treasure is, our heart is. And the heart of a disciple belongs to no one but God. A Christian admits no dependence on anything else. His only master is the Lord Jesus Christ.

Secular life is concerned frantically with escape—through novelty, variety, physical beauty, and possessions—from the fear of death. John Silber, president of Boston University, blasts what he sees as today's self-centered hedonism: "The gospel preached during every television show is 'You only go around once in life, so get all the gusto you can.' It is a statement about theology; it is a statement about beer. It's lousy beer and even worse theology."[6]

The teaching of Jesus on the uncluttered life and His injunction to travel light are well known: "Provide yourselves with no gold or silver, not even with a few coppers for your purses, with no haversack for the journey or spare tunic or footwear or a staff" (Matthew 10:9–10, JB). Do not worry "about your life and what you are to eat, nor about your body and how you are to clothe it" (Luke 12:22, JB). In the same chapter Jesus depicts a man who is busy building bigger barns and calls him a fool. All these sayings are cautions, loving encouragement from Jesus not to get distracted, waylaid, and ambushed by stuff that moth and rust consume and that has no enduring value. A Christian's simplicity of life is striking proof that he has found what he seeks, that he has stumbled onto the treasure hidden in the field.

This is one dimension of simplicity that Jesus proposes boldly and frequently for would-be disciples. Another dimension is its contrast with complexity. A favorite slogan in Alcoholics Anonymous is K.I.S.S.—"Keep it Simple, Stupid"—meaning don't complicate this simple but demanding program for sobriety.

Our lives in the global village have grown overcomplex and overcrowded. New obligations seem to grow overnight like Jack's beanstalk. Our days become a never-ending succession of appointments, committee meetings, burdens, and responsibilities. We are too busy to smell the flowers, to waste time with our spouses, to befriend our children, to cultivate true friends, or to be friends to those who have no friends. Our kids' schools demand our time, the civic problems of our community need our attention. Our professional status, our playtime, our membership in various organizations stake their claims. We run around like Lancelot's horse in four directions at once.

Weary and breathless, we sense that life is slipping away. We change our wardrobe, slip into the costume for the next performance and regret that we have tasted so little of the peace and joy that Jesus promised. What of prayer, silence, solitude, and simple presence to the indwelling God? Well, I'll get around to it but not today. This week is just too full.

The fallacy here is blaming the complexity of our lives on the complexity of our environment. How many people have told me they would love to live on some remote South Sea island or get back to the good old horse-and-buggy days when Sunday was spent visiting Grandma and Grandpa on the farm. *It doesn't work* because we bring our feverish, unintegrated selves to these remote places. Simplicity of life does not depend upon simplicity of environment.

The real problem lies within. Outer distractions reflect a lack of inner integration. "We are trying to be several selves at once. There is the civic self, the parental self, the financial self, the spiritual self, the society self, the professional self. And yet we are uneasy, strained, and fearful that we are shallow."[7] Driving along the turnpike or sitting in front of the TV, there comes a whispered call to the abundant life we have been neglecting: "Come to the water and slake your thirst." It is a hint that there is a way of life more satisfying than our hurried pace. We all know

81

people who seem to have mastered the pressures and stress of life, who don't feel guilty about saying no; in fact they say it with the same confidence as yes. They are no moony-eyed mystics but busy people carrying the same full load we are—but unhurried, unworried with a gleam in their eye and a spring in their step. While we are tense and uptight, they are poised and at peace.

If following Jesus has anything to say to us in the real world in which we live, it speaks to us right here. Our life in Christ is meant to be lived out of the Center. Lodged within us is the power to live a life of peace, integration, and confidence. The sole requirement for tapping it is *intensity of desire.* If you really want to live out of the Center, you will. We have all heard the gentle whisper of the Spirit in our lives. At times we have followed the whisper, and the result was amazing equilibrium of life, joy, energy and greater clarity of mind. Our outward life became simplified on the basis of inner integration.

Dominique Voillaume yielded to the Center and his life became simple. It had singleness of vision. "All that is not the love of God has no meaning for me." Much of our activity seems important to us. The six o'clock news is a command performance. An hour at the vanity table is like an audience with the Pope. We can't say no because these events seem indispensable. But if we "center down," as the old phrase goes, and take our daily agenda into the silent places of the heart with honesty, openness, and willingness, much of our activity loses its vitality and inviolability.

For a moment let me speak intimately about Jesus, whose love is dearer than life itself. Do you really want to live your life in His presence? Do you long for Him? Does every drop of blood in your body crave Him?

Let us suppose it were so ordained that your eternal destiny was to depend on your personal relationship with the bishop of your diocese. Would you not arrange to spend a little more time with him than you presently do? Wouldn't you strive to prove worthy of his friendship? Wouldn't you try assiduously to eliminate all personality traits displeasing to him from your life? When duties and obligations called you away from his presence, wouldn't you be eager to return to him as "the deer longs for the springs of running water"?

And if the bishop confided to you that he kept a diary of personal memoirs that were the deepest whisperings of his inner self, wouldn't you be anxious not only to read but to steep yourself in them so that you might know and love him more?

There are certain questions that every Christian must answer in utter candor. Do you hunger for Jesus Christ? Do you yearn to spend time alone with Him in prayer? Is He the most important person in your life? Does He fill your soul like a song of joy? Is He on your lips as a shout of praise? Do you eagerly turn to His memoirs, His Testament, to learn more of Him? Are you making the effort to die daily to anything and everything that inhibits, threatens, or diminishes your friendship?

To discern where you really are with the Lord, recall what *saddened* you the past week. Was it the realization that you don't love Jesus enough? That you neglected opportunities to show compassion for another? Or did you get depressed over lack of recognition, criticism from an authority figure, finances, lack of friends, fears about the future, your bulging waistline?

Conversely, what *gladdened* you the past week? Reflection on your election to the *ekklesia*? The joy of slowly praying, "Abba, Father"? The afternoon you stole away for an hour with the Scriptures as your only companion? A small victory over selfishness? Or were the sources of your joy a new car, a Brooks Brothers suit, a movie and a pizza, a trip to Paris or Peoria? Are you worshiping idols?

When disciples surrender to the mystery of the fire of

the Spirit that burns within, when we submit to the truth that we reach life only through death, when we acknowledge that the grain of wheat must vanish into the ground, that Jonah must be buried in the belly of the whale, that the alabaster jar of self must be broken if others are to perceive the sweet fragrance of Christ, when we respond to the call of Jesus, which is not come to church or a prayer meeting but "Come to Me," then the limitless power of the Holy Spirit will be unleashed with astonishing force. The *discipline of the secret* will be a compelling sign to the Church and the culture. The term *charismatic renewal* will fall into disuse. The *ekklesia* will be plunged into a revolution.

Clearly discipleship is a revolutionary way of living. A life lived in simplicity for God and others is what Paul had in mind when he wrote in Ephesians 4:23, "Your mind must be renewed by a spiritual revolution so that you can put on the new self that has been created in God's way, in the goodness and holiness of the truth" (JB).

Personally I take great comfort in the life stories of the first disciples. Their response was flawed by fear and hesitation. What they shared in common was dullness, an embarrassing inability to understand what Jesus was all about. Their track record was not good: They complained, they misunderstood, they quarreled, they wavered, they deserted, they denied. Christ's reaction to their broken, inconsistent discipleship was one of unending love. The Good News is that Jesus Christ is the same yesterday, today, and forever.

Five

Paschal Spirituality

In William Bausch's splendid book, *Storytelling, Imagination and Faith,* he recounts the following story:

An old Mississippi country preacher believed in his bones that the Word of God is a two-edged sword. One Sunday morning he mounted the pulpit and prayed: "Oh, Lord, give Thy servant this mornin' the eyes of the eagle and the wisdom of the owl; connect his soul with the gospel telephone in the central skies; illuminate his brow with the Sun of Heaven; possess his mind with love for the people; turpentine his imagination, grease his lips with possum oil; electrify his brain with the lightnin' of the Word; put perpetual motion in his arms; fill him plumb full of the dynamite of Thy glory; anoint him all over with the kerosene of salvation, and set him on fire. Amen!"[1]

Amen, indeed! Jesus did not come to bring peace but

the sword, not nightgowns but the armor of God. The Kingdom of God is not a matter of words but of power, a source of transformation and information. The spiritual life is simply life itself lived with the vision of faith. Any spirituality claiming the name Christian must resonate with the life and teaching of the Master.

The New Testament writings are the constituents of the early Church. They establish the essential characteristics of the apostolic community. The *ekklesia* of the '80s tries to conform to them. What is central in the New Testament should be central in the life of the Church today. Whatever is fringe or peripheral in the New Testament should not be made central today. (Thus any preoccupation with the gift of tongues is according undue weight to a marginal matter.) Jesus Christ in the mystery of His death and resurrection is the center of the New Testament from Matthew's genealogy to Revelation's "Maranatha." His breakthrough from death to life (*pesach* in Hebrew) is the core of the Gospel proclamation and the entire Christian faith. Therefore it can be unequivocally stated: To understand the paschal mystery is to understand Christianity; to be ignorant of the paschal mystery is to be ignorant of Christianity.

There is one spirituality in the *ekklesia* of the Lord Jesus. It is *paschal*, and there ain't any other. Paschal spirituality flows out of the paschal mystery. Essentially it is our daily death to sin, selfishness, dishonesty, and degraded love in order to rise to newness of life. Jesus continues His Pasch in the dying and rising of the members of His Body. Paul says, "It is no longer I who live, but Christ lives in me" (Galatians 2:20, NAS). Each time we deal a mortal blow to the ego, the Pasch of Jesus is traced in our flesh. Each time we choose to walk the extra mile, to turn the other cheek, to embrace and not reject, to be compassionate and not competitive, to kiss and not to bite, to forgive and not massage the latest bruise to our wounded ego, we are living the *pesach* of Jesus and breaking through from death to life.

The biblical word for conversion is *metanoia* meaning a radical transformation of our inner self. We discover that a personal relationship with Jesus Christ can no longer be contained in a code of do's and don't's. It becomes, as Jeremiah wrote, a covenant written in the fleshy tablets of the heart and inscribed in the depths of our being. Conversion opens us to a new agenda, new priorities, a different hierarchy of values. It stretches us from professing Jesus as Savior to confessing Him as Lord, from a mindless accommodation of our faith in our culture to a lived faith in the consuming truth of the Gospel. It "turpentines our imagination, electrifies our brain with the lightnin' of the Word, fills us plumb full of the dynamite of His glory and anoints us all over with the kerosene of salvation and sets us on fire."

"The opposite of conversion is aversion. The other side of metanoia is paranoia. Paranoia is usually understood in psychological terms. It is characterized by fear, suspicion, and flight from reality. Paranoia usually results in elaborate illusions and self-deception. In the biblical context paranoia implies more than emotional or mental imbalance. It refers to an attitude of being, a stance of the heart. Spiritual paranoia is a flight from God and from my true self. It is an attempt to escape from personal responsibility. It is the tendency to avoid the cost of discipleship and to seek out an escape route from the demands of the Gospel. Paranoia of the spirit is an attempt to deny the reality of Jesus in such a way that we rationalize our behavior and choose our own way."[2]

Each of us lives in the tension between metanoia and paranoia. We walk the narrow ridge between fidelity and betrayal. None of us is immune to the seduction of counterfeit discipleship. A watered-down Gospel would allow us to have the best of both worlds, a life of gilded mediocrity wherein we carefully distribute ourselves be-tween flesh and spirit with a watchful eye on both. The gospel of cheap grace dilutes faith into a lukewarm mix of Bible, nationalism, and compromise—a spirituality that bears no resemblance to the paschal mystery.

What are the characteristics of true paschal spirituality? There are seven of them:

First, it is *Christocentric*. It is through Christ, with Christ, and in Christ. This may seem so self-evident that it hardly merits our attention. But Christian history, both past and present, is the ongoing story of a tragic distortion when Jesus Christ ceases to be the center of the Christian life. In the past, certain devotional practices have received so much attention in thought and preaching that direct devotion to the person of Jesus Christ in and through the *ekklesia* has taken second place. In other Christian circles the tendency to "absolutize" certain sections of the New Testament (for instance, Acts 1–3 and 1 Corinthians 12–14) has placed the emphasis on peak religious experiences and spectacular gifts of the Spirit—with the result that the paschal mystery has been relegated to the margins of Christian faith and practice.

In the present decade, preoccupation with styles of worship—traditional or renewed, organ or guitar, hymns or choruses, incense or balloons, recited or spontaneous prayers, old or new translations of the Bible—have up-staged the central drama of Calvary and Easter morning. Style overshadows substance, form transcends content, the Church supplants Jesus. As we said earlier, a Chris-tian's right thinking is the new standard for determining what he or she is or is not worth in the sight of God and everyone else.

Above the din the Abba of Jesus cries out: "You go to church every Sunday and read your Bible, but the Body of My Son is broken. You memorize chapter and verse and honor all your traditions, but the Body of My Son is broken. You recite the creed and defend orthodoxy, but the Body of My Son is broken. You hark back to tradition and press forward toward renewal, but the Body of My Son is broken."

At this point in Church history I believe it is imperative to remember that the Christ of John's Gospel asked Peter (who had denied him three times) only one question: "Do you love Me?" The criterion by which the Johannine Christ measures His friends and repudiators is still "Do you love Me?" What is the good of Bible study, reform, and renewal if we forget this, even if we hold to everything else? How can anyone muster the incredible hardheartedness and the intemperate messianic zeal to inflate style and tradition, orthodoxy, biblical interpretation, and right thinking into such a monster that Jesus' question to Peter and us is put on the shelf?

The author of the fourth Gospel puts but one question to his readers: Do we know Jesus? To know Him is life. Everything else fades into twilight and darkness. For the evangelist John, what constitutes dignity in the Christian community is not apostleship or office, not titles or charisms, not the gifts of prophecy, healing, or inspired preaching, but only intimacy with Jesus. This is a status that all Christians enjoy.

To our contemporary Church, which treats chief administrative officials and charismatic superstars with excessive deference, the Gospel of John sends this prophetic word: The love of Jesus Christ alone gives status in the Christian community. In his powerful pastoral book *The Churches the Apostles Left Behind,* the Johannine scholar Raymond Brown writes: "All Christians are disciples and among them greatness is determined by a loving relationship with Jesus, not by function or office. Church offices and even apostleship are of lesser importance when compared to discipleship, which is literally a question of eternal life or death. Within that discipleship, there are no second-class Christians."[3]

The thrust of paschal spirituality is Christocentric. It

never loses sight of the Johannine Christ's question "Do you love Me?" nor does it try to go the Master one better. Even if everything is in confusion, nothing is finally ruined as long as disciples will still follow Him, be held fast by Him, learn from Him, and love Him.

Three years ago, a white prisoner died of a heart attack in a Montgomery, Alabama, jail. While in prison he had had a profound conversion experience and entered into an authentic relationship with Jesus. The convict in the next cell, a huge black, was a cynic. Each night the white prisoner spoke through the prison bars and told him about the love of Jesus. The black mocked him, told him he was sick in the head, that religion was the last refuge of the insane. Nonetheless, the white passed Scripture passages to him and shared his candy whenever he received a gift from a relative. At the white man's funeral service, when the prison chaplain spoke of the Easter victory of Jesus, the burly black stood up in the middle of the sermon, pointed to the coffin, and said, "That's the only Jesus I ever knew."

Paschal spirituality says that if our Christian journey does not produce Christ in us, if the passing years do not form Jesus in us in such a way that we really resemble Him, spirituality is bankrupt. Once again, we witness the power in the "discipline of the secret": quietly dying daily to self so that the risen Christ may live more fully in us.

A second characteristic of paschal spirituality is that it is *communitarian*. A deep awareness of the social nature of salvation is an ineluctable consequence of this spirituality. For the Christian has risen in Christ as a member of His Body. We belong to God's people. Christianity can never be an affair that simply embraces our individual happiness. Paschal spirituality avoids any exaggerated form of Christian individualism—a "Jesus and me" mentality that becomes individualistic to the point that a sense of the *ekklesia* is lost and membership in the Christian community becomes almost irrelevant. God did not call us into salvation in isolation but in community. Our personal destiny is but part of His magnificent saving plan that includes in its sweep not only the entire human community but the whole of creation, the inauguration of the new heavens and the new earth.

The loss of a paschal spirituality has preempted fraternal love as the distinctive mark of discipleship. The "Jesus and me" mindset tells us that all we have to do is accept Christ as Savior, read the Bible, go to church, and save our souls. Christianity becomes a kind of telephone booth affair, a private conversation between God and me without reference to my brothers and sisters. I go to church on Sunday while the world goes to hell. When preoccupation with my personal salvation drugs me into such insensitivity that I no longer hear the bleating of the lost sheep, then Karl Marx was right: Religion is the opium of the people.

One dislocating, self-impoverishing hour spent by a Christian with a little child living in a broken-down dump on a heartless street—such an hour is worth more than all the burial mounds of rhetoric, all the enfeebled good intentions, all the mumbling and fumbling and tardiness of those Christians who are so busy cultivating their own holiness that they cannot hear the anguished cry of the child in the slum.

The Christian life is meant to be lived in community. And community life is a radical imitation of the holy and undivided Trinity who is dialogue, spontaneous love, and relationship. "No one has ever seen God; but as long as we love one another God will live in us and his love will be complete in us" (1 John 4:12, JB). Paschal spirituality insists that to love one another means the love of God has reached full growth in our lives.

"A Gentile once came to Rabbi Shammai and said, 'Convert me to Judaism on condition that you can teach me the whole Torah while I am standing on one foot.'

With a rod in his hand Rabbi Shammai angrily threw him out. Then the man went to Rabbi Hillel and repeated his request. 'Convert me to Judaism on condition that you can teach me the whole Torah while I am standing on one foot.' Rabbi Hillel converted him and taught him as follows: 'What is hateful to you, do not do to your neighbor.' This is the whole Torah. All the rest is commentary."[4]

Paul says that he who loves his neighbor has fulfilled the entire Law and the prophets (Romans 13:10). The words of Charles deFoucaulds, "One learns to love God by loving men and women," surge from the very heart of the Christian tradition. This is the mind of Christ. The eclipse of fraternal love as the foremost sign of discipleship has led to the divisive individualism and splintering of the twentieth-century Church. Christianity has been cleaned and pressed so often in the clanking machines of hypocrisy that we think it belongs to the proper and pious, to those who stand at a safe distance from the back alleys of existence, clucking their judgments at those who have been soiled by life. What has been the Christian reaction to the stained life of the late Rock Hudson and the disclosure that he prayed to God on his deathbed? Is there room in the kingdom of our hearts for a fallen homosexual? If so, is there room for those who do not interpret the Bible the way we do?

Paschal spirituality says that the truest test of discipleship is the way we live with each other in the community of faith. It is as simple and as demanding as that. In our words and deeds we give shape and form to our faith every day. We make people a little better or leave them a little worse. We either affirm or deprive, enlarge or diminish the lives of others. "The Kingdom, Jesus tells us, is in our very midst, in the mystery of our relationships with each other. We are within its gates when we draw close to one another with the love that is fired by the Spirit. We are already on sacred ground when we reach out to understand rather than condemn, when we forgive rather than seek revenge, when as unarmed pilgrims we are ready to meet our enemies. What Jesus teaches is too simple and too wonderful for those who want magic in their religion."[5]

According to the evangelical criterion for holiness, the person closest to the heart of Jesus Christ is not the one who prays the most, studies Scripture the most, or the one who has the most important position of spiritual responsibility entrusted to his or her care. It is the one who loves the most, and that is not my opinion. It is the Word that will judge us.

A third characteristic of paschal spirituality: *It views people as basically good.* Paschal spirituality is freed of all Manichaean influence, the dualistic heresy that saw the body as enemy and the soul as friend. Paschal spirituality looks upon human nature as fallen but redeemed, flawed but in essence good. The whole person, body, mind, and spirit, is risen with Christ through water and the Spirit. The body is a sacred vessel, a shrine of the imperishable Spirit. The emotions are good needing only direction and grace, not suppression. We are Christians, not Stoics. We could do with a good deal less of the pessimism found in some Christian circles regarding earthy things. The moderate use of alcohol, cosmetics, dancing, laughter, and human affection are basically good. Creation is the overflow of the goodness of God and His infinite love.

In response to the question "Why did God make the world?" paschal spirituality replies that God the Father had this thing about being. As Robert Capon put it (in a quotation for which I long ago lost the source):

"He was absolutely wild about being. He kept thinking up new ways of being and new kinds of being to be. One afternoon, God the Son came along and said: 'This is really great stuff. Why don't I go out and mix up a batch?' And God the Holy Spirit said, 'Terrific! I'll help you.'

"So they got together that night after supper and put on

a tremendous show of being for the Father. It was full of water and light and frogs; pussywillows kept dropping all over the place, and speckled fish swam around in the wine glasses. There were mushrooms and grapes, horseradishes and tigers—and men and women everywhere to taste them, juggle them, join with them, and love them. God the Father looked at the whole wild party and said, 'Wonderful. Just what I had in mind. Yeh!' And all God the Son and Holy Spirit could think of was to say, 'Yeh, yeh!' They laughed for ages saying things like how great it was for being to be, how clever of the Father to conceive the idea, how kind of the Son to go to all the trouble to put it together, and how gracious of the Spirit to devote so much time to choreography. They told old jokes to one another and the Father and Son drank their wine in the unity of the Holy Spirit and threw ripe olives and pickled mushrooms at each other forever and ever."

Admittedly this is a crass analogy, but perhaps crass analogies are the safest. Everyone knows that God is not a bearded old man throwing olives. But not everyone is convinced that God is not merely a "cosmic force," an "uncaused cause," an "immovable mover," or any of the other analogies we use about Him. The image of creation as the result of a hilarious Trinitarian bash might be bonkers, but it does hint at the truth that God takes delight in His creation.

Creation, Genesis says, is good. Created things are just so many myriad responses to the delight of God who wills them into being. Thomas Aquinas said being is good in itself. Being and good are interchangeable.

Of course, it is not always easy to see that all being is good. Affirming our faith in the goodness of creation becomes problematic in the face of the earthquake in Mexico City that claimed 5,000 lives, or the mudslide in Colombia that killed 40,000. In addition, as Capon notes, there are poison toadstools, cancer cells, liver flukes, killer whales, and loan sharks to be considered. But there is no retreating from the revelation in Genesis: "God looked at everything He had made and found it very good."

The human person is basically good. Human nature, freed from the slavery of sin, is capable of awesome holiness. Evangelist Robert Frost in an address in San Jose, California, remarked, "The Lord brought me up short with the challenge: 'Why do you persist in seeing your children in the hands of the devil, rather than in the arms of their faithful Shepherd?' I then realized that in my mind I had been imagining the evils of the present age as being more powerful than the timeless love of God."

Paschal spirituality recovers the element of delight in creation. Imagine the ecstasy, the cry of joy when God makes a person in His own image! When God made you! The Father gives you as a gift to Himself. You are a response to the vast delight of God. Out of an infinite number of possibilities God invested you and me with existence.

Have I really appreciated the wondrous gift that I am? Or do I measure my worth by the texture of my hair, the structure of my face, the size of my waistline? Could the Father's gift to Himself be anything but beautiful? I sing of His other gifts—"girls in white dresses with blue satin sashes, snowflakes that stay on my nose and eye-lashes. . . ."[6] Why don't I like my beautiful self? Paschal spirituality says that because of the death and resurrection of Jesus Christ I can love myself not in spite of my flaws and warts but with them. Such is the total acceptance of the God of Jesus.

Next, paschal spirituality is *stamped with the signature of Jesus*. There is no genuine Christianity where the sign of the cross is absent. Cheap grace is grace without the cross, an intellectual assent to a dusty pawnshop of doctrinal beliefs while drifting aimlessly with the cultural values of the secular city. Discipleship without sacrifice breeds comfortable Christianity barely distinguishable in its mediocrity from the rest of the world. The cross is both the test and the destiny of a follower of Christ.

"What we desperately need to reunderstand is that it is dangerous to be a true Christian. Anyone who takes his or her Christianity seriously will realize that crucifixion is not something that happened to one man nineteen hundred and fifty-odd years ago, nor was martyrdom just the fate of his early followers. It should be an omnipresent risk for every Christian. Christians should—need—in certain ways to live dangerously if they are to live out their faith. The times have made this apparent. Today the times demand of us that we take major risks for peace. And in combating the entrenched forces of the arms race—the principalities and powers of this world—that very much includes the risk of martyrdom. . . . It is time for communal, congregational action and corporate risk."[7]

Tepid preaching and lifeless worship have spread so many ashes on the fire of the Gospel that we scarcely feel the glow anymore. We have gotten so used to the ultimate Christian fact—Jesus naked, stripped, and crucified—that we no longer see it for what it is: a summons to strip ourselves of earthly cares and worldly wisdom, all desire for human praise, greediness for any kind of comfort (spiritual consolations included); a readiness to stand up and be counted as peacemakers in a violent world; a willingness to let go of those pretenses that would have us believe that we really aren't worldly (the kind of worldliness that prefers the more attractive duty to the less attractive, which puts us to more effort for people we want to stand well with). Even the last rag we cling to—the self-flattery that suggests we are being humble when we disclaim any resemblance to Jesus Christ—even that rag has to go when we stand face-to-face with the crucified Son of God.

Charles Colson, Watergate crook and wheeler-dealer

par excellence, is a magnificent witness to many aspects of paschal spirituality. His awareness of salvation-in-community speaks for itself through his prison ministry. In addition, his life is a lovely letter to God signed with the signature of Jesus. Recently he learned that he has a malignant cancer. He thought he would be shattered but he discovered in his confrontation with fear and suffering that there is nothing for which God does not pour out His grace abundantly. The tumor was caught early and doctors have assured him that the prognosis is excellent. Colson says:

"My suffering provided some fresh insights . . . into the health-and-wealth gospel. If God really delivers his people from all pain and illness, as is so often claimed, why was I so sick? Had my faith become weak? Had I fallen from favor? No, I had always recognized such teaching as false theology. But after four weeks in a maximum care unit, I came to see it as something else: a presumptuous stumbling block to real evangelism." Dragging his I.V. pole down a hospital corridor, Colson was asked by a Hindu visiting his desperately ill son whether or not God would heal the boy if he, the father, were to be born again. "He said he had heard things like that on television. As I listened, I realized how arrogant health-and-wealth religion sounds to suffering families. Christians can be spared suffering but little Hindu children go blind. One couldn't blame a Hindu or Muslim or agnostic for resenting, even hating, such a God." As for his cancer, "We don't begin to know all the reasons why. But we do know that our suffering and weakness can be an opportunity to witness to the world the amazing grace of God at work through us."[8]

Paschal spirituality is nothing less than bondage to Jesus Christ alone, a complete attachment to His Person, a sharing in the rhythm of His death and resurrection, a participation in His life of sorrow, rejection, loneliness, and suffering. To paraphrase Francis Thompson: "The wood must be charred before He can limn with it."

A fifth dimension of paschal spirituality: *It is joyful and optimistic.* It is solidly anchored in the virtue of hope. It eagerly looks forward to the final glorification of the Parousia. The cry of the Christian is, "There's gonna be a great day." The faithful God who completed Israel's Pasch by leading them into the Promised Land will complete the Christian Pasch by leading us into the promised land of glory where the victory of Jesus Christ will shine like a neon light in the skies and angelic trumpets will announce the final harvest. The true Christian is the lover separated from his beloved; the day of reunion cannot come too soon. Such is the happy, hopeful, buoyant spirit that characterizes paschal spirituality. It should set the tone of our life in Christ day by day.

Eugene O'Neill once wrote a muddled play with a splendid ending. It dealt with the life of Lazarus after Jesus summoned him from the grave. O'Neill called his play *Lazarus Laughed.* It is the story of a lover of Jesus who had tasted death and seen it for what it is. "Laugh with me! Death is dead! Fear is no more! There is only life! There is only laughter!" And O'Neill tells us: Lazarus begins to laugh, softly at first, then full-throated: "A laugh so full of complete acceptance of life, a profound assertion of joy in living, so devoid of all fear, that it is infectious with love, so infectious that, despite themselves, his listeners are caught up by it and carried away."

"Laughter is not hysteria. Laughter is not a belly explosion over a vulgar joke. Laughter is . . . joy in living." Paschal spirituality says to the Christian: You can laugh, you can take delight in living. Why? "Because in the midst of death you are constantly discovering life: in a glance or a touch or a song, in a field of corn or a friend who cares, in the moon or an amoeba, in a lifeless loaf suddenly become the body of Christ."[9] Laughter is splendidly human, utterly Christian, deeply paschal.

Paschal spirituality proclaims that death is an illusion

and that Jesus came primarily as a man of hope, a paschal man, an eschatological man, and indeed as a personal eschaton.

Here is the root and source of Christian joy, mirth, and laughter. It is why theologian Robert Hotchkins can insist: "Christians ought to be celebrating constantly. We ought to be preoccupied with parties, banquets, feasts, and merriment. We ought to give ourselves over to veritable orgies of joy because of our belief in resurrection. We ought to attract people to our faith quite literally by the fun there is in being a Christian. Unfortunately, however, we too readily become somber, serious, and pompous. We fly in the face of our own tradition because we are afraid of wasting time or getting attached. In the words of Teresa of Avila, 'from silly devotions and sour-faced saints, spare us, O Lord.' "

No one has educated people to the meaning of merriment and joy like Jesus and His *ekklesia*. It was the Church standing alone in the fourth century that resolutely insisted, in the face of the Manichaean heresy, that the body and the physical world around us are not only good but through the paschal mystery have become better. Jesus' presence at the wedding feast of Cana and His miracle work to keep the party going are the definitive Christian answer to all the prohibitionists, party poopers, and puritans who have appeared on the scene since that memorable gathering in Galilee. Christianity is not Jansenism. Hilaire Belloc's oft-quoted phrase captures the joyful character of paschal spirituality: "Wherever a Christian sun doth shine, there's always laughter and good red wine. At least I've always found it so, Benedicamus Domino!"

The paschal victory of Jesus Christ presents us with only two logical alternatives: Either you believe in the resurrection, and hence you believe in Jesus of Nazareth and the Gospel He preached; or you believe in non-resurrection, and you do not believe in Jesus of Nazareth and the Gospel He preached. If Easter is not history, we must become cynics. In other words, either we believe in resurrection and a living Jesus who is with us in faith and we commit our lives to both, or we do not. Either we dismiss the Good News as too good to be true, or we permit ourselves to be overwhelmed by its joyfulness and become overwhelmingly joyful persons because of it. A Christian is called to believe in a God who loves and His Christ who is risen. We believe and we believe strongly; we believe and we believe joyously.

Joy in the risen Jesus is directly connected with the quality of our faith, for a sad Christian is not really an authentic Christian, and a guilty Christian is no Christian at all. Mother Teresa has chosen to live her life among the most afflicted of God's children, yet she can say: "Never let anything so fill your heart with grief that you forget the joy of the risen Lord."

Ignatius of Loyola encourages paschal Christians to pray often for the *charism of intense gladness*.[10] This is not giddy, cocktail party gaiety or a brave attempt to smile through the tears. It is a deep-seated gladness rooted in the victory and promise of the risen Jesus. Compassion, the ability to suffer with the hurt of another, is an essential Christian quality. Equally important is the capacity to rejoice in the happiness of another. Intense gladness is anchored in the joy that Christ now experiences at the right hand of His Father. Every tear has been wiped away. There is no more mourning or sadness in the life of the risen Jesus.

When this gift of intense gladness is given, it produces a joy that is solid and impregnable, rooted deep beneath the shifting sands of our fickle feelings. Whatever happens, the Lord is risen! Nothing can suffocate this joy and hope. Whether the day is stormy or fair, whether I am sick or in good health, nothing alters the fact that Christ is risen. In the early Church, each Sunday was known as the feast of "little Easter." In our own culture the Christian Sabbath is a summons to the joy and optimism of paschal spirituality.

The sixth aspect of this spirituality: *It promotes unity without uniformity.* Jesus is the Way, and His light is refracted in myriad ways by different personalities. He incarnates Himself in new and surprising ways in each of us. Each of us is called to be a unique and singular manifestation of Christ's truth and love, not a carbon copy of someone else. In paschal spirituality there is no attempt to cast people into a certain mold, but rather a readiness to recognize the rich variety of persons and personalities who blend together to make up the *ekklesia.* No effort is made to destroy the wealth of variety in a drive for sameness. In terms of church worship, the operative principle is unity in praising God without uniformity in style.

Finally, paschal spirituality *regards persons as free.* We are a free people by virtue of the freedom with which Christ has made us free. As Paul writes, "With the new law freedom comes." Christians are to be treated by religious authorities as free men and women, not slaves. We are responsible human beings with the ability to make rational decisions. Enlightened (not blind) obedience is the paschal ideal. There is ready acceptance of the truth that each person's destiny lies in his own hands, guided and strengthened by the grace of Christ. There is profound awareness that the fundamental secret of Jesus was His sovereign respect for human liberty. He never tried to make people virtuous against their will. This is the essential betrayal.

The institutional Church is untrue to the law of its own being whenever it violates freedom. Whenever any authority figure, be it Pope, patriarch, bishop, priest, minister, or parent seeks to suppress freedom, he or she is thereby setting himself (however unconsciously) in opposition to Christ and His Church. God created human persons in His own image because He wanted free, responsible service. When the virtue of obedience is reduced to a pattern of domination and submission, we produce trained cowards rather than Christian persons.

I want for myself a spirituality of passion, intelligence, and creative freedom rooted in the paschal mystery. And I cannot write these words dispassionately. After twenty-six years of celibate priesthood, I chose freely to marry Roslyn because I love her and because I felt God calling me to walk hand-in-hand with her for the remainder of my journey. Our covenant has been declared illicit and invalid by the hierarchical Church. I have been stripped of faculties to preach the Gospel and celebrate the sacraments. Life is too short, however, for nursing resentments or munching sour grapes. In the gathering mist of middle age, I am losing my taste for controversy and crusades. I merely suggest in passing that the time has come for change in the discipline of the Roman Catholic Church.

Perhaps this is the hardest lesson of paschal spirituality—to look upon ourselves and others as free, responsible persons. Instead of creating more freedom, all of us unwittingly erect impediments to it, impediments such as neurotic fear, pressure, threats of punishment. The tragedy of our attempts to compel others to be virtuous by force or subtle manipulation is that these efforts are so prevalent in our lives, so characteristic of our relationships with others that most of us, most of the time, are unaware of the problem. We do not perceive that we betray a basic lack of respect for the humanity of those with whom we deal, and that this lack of respect is the essential problem with the use of authority in the church and in the home.

If we really knew the God of Jesus, we would stop trying to control and manipulate others "for their own good," knowing full well that this is not how God works among His people. Paul writes: "Where the Spirit of the Lord is, there is freedom" (2 Corinthians 3:17, NIV).

These are the central features and dominant characteristics of paschal spirituality centered in the life, death, and resurrection of Jesus Christ. Death and resurrection are not one-time events that occur only at the end of our journey. They are the pattern of our lives day after day. "Each time we let go of the past to embrace the future we relive the paschal journey of Jesus in our flesh. Each time we allow our fears or selfishness to die, we break through to new life. Each time we open ourselves to the Spirit so that he can break down the walls of suspicion and bitterness, we come home to ourselves, the community and the Lord. 'I die daily,' Paul wrote. He might have added, 'And daily I am raised up to new life.' "[11]

To write the letter of our lives over the signature of Jesus is to recognize His dying and rising as they are traced in our actions and carved in our hearts. In such a context, death will not be a new experience for us, nor will resurrection!

Six

Celebrate
the Darkness

"A certain Christian thought it was of vital importance to be poor and austere. It had never dawned on him that the vitally important thing was to drop his ego; that the ego fattens on holiness just as much as on worldliness, on poverty as on riches, on austerity as on luxury. There is nothing the ego will not seize upon to inflate itself.

"Disciple: I have come to you with nothing in my hands.

"Master: Then drop it at once!

"Disciple: But how can I drop it? It is nothing.

"Master: Then carry it around with you! You can make a possession of your nothing. And carry your renunciation around you like a trophy. Don't drop your possessions. Drop your ego."[1]

Paschal spirituality (death to self in order to live for

God) requires a crucifixion of the ego. That is why mature Christian prayer inevitably leads to the purification of "the dark night of the senses and the spirit" through loneliness and aridity, which buries egoism and leads us out of ourselves to experience God. The signature of Jesus, the sign of the cross, is writ large on the interior life of every authentic disciple.

The "dark night" is a very real place, as anyone who has been there will tell you. Alan Jones calls it "the second conversion." While the first conversion was characterized by joy and enthusiasm and filled with felt consolation and a profound sense of God's presence, the second is marked by dryness, barrenness, desolation, and a profound sense of God's absence. The dark night is an indispensable stage of spiritual growth both for the individual Christian and the *ekklesia*. Merton writes, "There is an absolute need for the solitary, bare, dark, beyond-thought, beyond-feeling type of prayer. . . . Unless that dimension is there in the Church somewhere, the whole caboodle lacks life and light and intelligence. It is a kind of hidden, secret, unknown stabilizer and compass too. About this I have no hesitation or doubts. . . ."[2]

Though painful, the purification of the ego in the dark night is the high road to Christian freedom and maturity. In fact, it is often an answer to prayer.

Have you ever prayed that you might be more prayerful? Have you ever prayed for a lively and conscious awareness of God's indwelling presence throughout the day? Have you ever prayed that you might be gentle and humble in heart? Have you ever asked for a spirit of detachment from material things, personal relationships, and creature comforts? Have you ever cried out for an increase in faith? I know I have, and I suspect that we have all prayed often for these spiritual gifts. But I wonder if we really meant what we said when we asked for these things? Did we really want what we asked for? I think not.

Otherwise, why did we recoil in shock and sorrow when our prayers were answered?

The suffering involved in arriving at the answer made us sorry we ever asked in the first place. We asked for spiritual growth and Christian maturity but we really didn't want them—at least not in the way God chose to grant them.

For example, if we ask the Lord to make us more prayerful, how does He answer our prayer? By bringing us to our knees in adversity and suffering. Have you ever heard a Christian complain, "What's happened? The week after I was 'born again,' all hell broke loose. I lost my job and my car keys, quarreled with my wife, and got on the wrong plane and wound up in Philadelphia instead of San Francisco."

Through a sequence of human events (divinely inspired), the God and Father of our Lord Jesus Christ leads us into a state of interior devastation. When we are like this, it is highly probable (though not inevitable) that we become more prayerful. Up to now we had not been praying in depth; now we are truly praying. We might not be saying all that many prayers, and we might not be following the set formulas that we presumed were prayer, but we are praying as never before. God is drawing us closer to Himself. We ask, "What's happening?" And the answer comes: "Don't you remember? This is what you asked for. There is no cheap grace. You wanted to be more prayerful. Now you are."

Our original petition was to achieve a constant state of prayerfulness. Well, nothing inspires prayer like adversity, sorrow, and humiliation. In these broken times we pray at our best. Our prayer rises in utter simplicity: "Lord Jesus Christ, Son of God, I trust in You." Or, "Abba, I belong to You." In Catherine de Hueck Doherty's phrase, "We put our head into our heart and our cerebral short-sightedness is cured."

When we pray for the gift of a prayerful heart, the Lord

strips away any props we might lean on, and leads us into spiritual desolation, into the dark night of the soul in order that we might pray with a pure heart. As the second-century Shepherd of Hermas said: Let us be careful not to seek mystical experiences when we should be seeking repentance and conversion. That is the beginning of our cry to God: "Lord, make me what I should be, change me whatever the cost." And when we have said these dangerous words, we should be prepared for God to hear them. And these words are dangerous because God's love is remorseless. God wants our salvation with the determination due its importance. And, the Shepherd of Hermas, concludes, "God does not leave us until he has broken our hearts and our bones."[3]

Jesus says: "Learn from me, for I am gentle and humble in heart" (Matthew 11:29, NIV). These beautiful words are a portrait of the heart of Christ. So we respond, "Jesus, gentle and humble in heart, make my heart like Yours." Now we are really in for it. We have just opened Pandora's box. Why? Because we don't learn humility by reading about it in spiritual books or listening to its praises in sermons. We learn humility directly from the Lord Jesus in whatever way He wishes to teach us. Most often we learn humility through humiliations. What is humility? It is the stark realization and acceptance of the fact that I am totally dependent upon God's love and mercy. It grows through a stripping away of all self-sufficiency. Humility is not caught by repeating pious phrases. It is accomplished by the hand of God. It is Job on the dunghill all over again as God reminds us that He is our only true hope.

I know a man who felt comfortably close to Christ for thirty years because his ministry had been a success. He had made his mark, produced good work, was respected and esteemed by the community. It seemed as though his success was the reward for his faithfulness. Then one day God took pity on him and granted his prayer to be humble in heart. What happened?

In a blinding moment of truth, the man saw his ministerial success as riddled with vanity and self-seeking, ephemeral, empty. Soon friends drifted away; his popularity waned. He became conscious of distrust on the part of others. Radical differences developed on issues such as church growth and evangelism. Sickness brought inactivity and heightened the sense of loss.

The man entered the dark night. For the first time he experienced the unbearable absence of God in his life. He suspected that his life had been a disappointment to God, a disappointment he was powerless to undo. He felt he had lost Jesus through pride and selfishness. He was convinced that the rebuke of the divine Judge in the book of Revelation was aimed at him: "You say, how rich I am! And how well I have done! I have everything I want. In fact, though you do not know it, you are the most pitiful wretch, poor, blind, and naked."

The pain was excruciating, the dark night pitch-black. Later, however, when the man looked back on that painful experience of ego-reduction, he recognized that his agony was an answer to prayer, that the humiliation he endured was God's way of saying yes to his plea to be more like Jesus.

Biblically there is nothing more detestable than a self-sufficient person. He is so full of himself, so swollen with pride and conceit that he is insufferable. Here is a scenario that plays in my mind:

A humble woman seeks me out because of my renown as a spiritual guide. She is simple and direct. "Please teach me how to pray." Tersely, I inquire, "Tell me about your prayer life."

She lowers her eyes and says contritely, "There's not much to tell. I say grace before meals."

Haughtily, I reply, "You say grace before meals? Isn't that nice. Madam, I say grace upon waking and retiring and grace before reading the newspaper and turning on the television. I say grace before ambulating and defecating, before the theatre and the opera, before jogging, swimming, hiking, dining, lecturing, writing. I even say grace before I say grace!"

And God whispers to me: "You ungrateful turd. Even the desire to say grace is itself My gift."

There is an ancient Christian legend that goes this way:

"When the Son of God was nailed to the cross and gave up His Spirit, He went straight down to hell from the cross and set free all the sinners who were there in torment. And the Devil wept and mourned for he thought he would get no more sinners for hell.

"Then God said to him, 'Do not weep, for I shall send you all those holy people who have become self-complacent in the consciousness of their goodness and self-righteous in their condemnation of sinners. And hell shall be filled up once more for generations until I come again.' "[4]

Most of the time, the self-sufficient Christian is blind to his arrogant pretensions. Even prayer is used for self-justification. He goes along his merry way reciting pious little phrases like, "Jesus, keep me humble." And at last the God who cannot be manipulated or controlled replies, "Fine. You want to be humble, do you? This sequence of humiliations and failures will take care of that."

The school of humiliation is a great learning experience; there is no other like it. When the gift of a humble heart is granted, we are more accepting of ourselves and less critical of others. Self-knowledge brings a humble and realistic awareness of our limitations. It leads us to be patient and compassionate with others, whereas before we were demanding, insensitive, and stuck-up. Gone are the complacency and narrowmindedness that made God superfluous. For the humble person there is a constant awareness of his or her own weakness, insufficiency, and desperate need for God.

Probably the moment in my own life when I was closest

to the Truth who is Jesus Christ was the experience of being a hopeless derelict in the gutter in Fort Lauderdale, Florida. In his novel *The Moviegoer*, Walker Percy says: "Only once in my life was the grip of everydayness broken: when I lay bleeding in the ditch." Paradoxically, such an experience of powerlessness does not make one sad. It is a great relief because it makes us rely not on our own strength but on the limitless power of God. The realization that God is the main agent makes the yoke easy, the burden light, and the heart still.

Of course, the most withering experience of ego-reduction occurs when we pray, "Lord, increase my faith." We need to tread carefully here, because the life of pure faith *is* the dark night. In this "night" God allows us to live by faith and faith alone. Mature faith cannot grow when we are surfeited with all kinds of spiritual comforts and consolations. All these must be removed if we are to advance in the pure trust of God. The Lord withdraws all tangible supports to purify our hearts, to discern if we are in love with the gifts of the Giver or the Giver of the gifts.

"The question is, do I worship God or do I worship my experience of God? Do I worship God or do I worship my idea of him? If I am to avoid a narcotic approach to religion that forces me to stagger from experience to experience hoping for bigger and better things, I must *know* what I believe apart from the nice or nasty feelings that may or may not accompany such a belief. The second conversion has to do with learning to cope and flourish when the warm feelings, consolations, and props that accompany the first conversion are withdrawn. Does faith evaporate when the initial feelings dissolve? In psychological terms, the ego has to break; and this breaking is like entering into a *great darkness*. Without such a struggle and affliction, there can be no movement in love"[5] (italics mine).

The prayer for increased faith separates the men from the boys, the women from the girls, the mystics from the romantics. In her autobiography, the thirteenth-century mystic Catherine of Siena described her prayer life as glorious. She had a highly conscious awareness of the divine indwelling. She loved to spend days alone locked up in her room enjoying the felt presence of the beautiful God who dwelt in her heart. These were times of immense spiritual consolation, mountaintop experiences, moments of intimate personal encounter. There was peace, joy, security, certitude. God, her God, was always with her. Her life in the Spirit would be an unbroken upward spiral toward holiness. So she thought. . . .

Until one day her comfortable life in Christ exploded. She lost the familiar feelings of the secure possession of God. The indwelling Trinity, she felt, was gone. She lost the sense of His presence and felt dead to His influence. Even the memory of Him seemed unreal. God had vanished like last night's dream. Now the only thing that occupied her consciousness was sin. Impure images filled her thoughts and her body tingled in response. She felt as though she had been plunged into a pool of filth, and that she had lost forever her clean, joyous life with Christ. She was plunged into the dark night. But the darkness proved to be the matrix from which sprang light, grace, and growth in faith.

After a long period of dryness, emptiness, and aridity, without any preparation or warning, Catherine suddenly found Jesus again. She had a profound experience of His loving presence in the very room where she had been tempted so fiercely. Angrily she complained, "Lord, where were You when all those foul images tormented my mind?" The answer of Jesus led her into a new depth of faith. "Catherine, all during your temptations, I have remained with you in the depths of your heart. Otherwise, you could not have overcome them."

At that critical moment, Catherine of Siena surrendered forever her old concept of the presence of God. Jesus' words had taught her that His presence in her heart was something deeper and holier than she could imagine or feel. In this life He is always a hidden God. Human feelings cannot touch Him and human thoughts cannot measure Him. Personal experience cannot heighten the certainty of His presence any more than the absence of experience can lessen it. These words made Catherine realize as never before that nothing but grave, conscious, deliberate sin could separate her from the Beloved of her soul. Not noise, irritating people, distractions, or temptations, not feelings of consolation or desolation, not success or failure, nothing but turning back could ever separate her from the love of God made visible in Jesus Christ our Lord. He would always be there in the quiet darkness just as He promised: "Be not afraid, I will be with you." Catherine had lost the presence of God only to find it again in the "deep and dazzling darkness" of a richer faith. The dark night was an answered prayer. She was free to *celebrate the darkness*.

Our common tendency is to believe that when we no longer feel the presence and consolation of God, He is no longer there. Alan Jones summarizes the theology of St. John of the Cross regarding the dark night: "The first sign of the second conversion is that we no longer have any pleasure or consolation either in God or in creation. Nothing pleases us. Nothing touches us. Everything and everyone seem dull and uninteresting. Life is dust and ashes in the mouth. The second sign is an abiding and biting sense of failure, even though the believer conscientiously tries to center her life on God. There is a sense of never having done enough and of needing to atone for something that has no name.

"The third sign, and the one that is most threatening to us today, is that it is no longer possible to pray or meditate with the imagination. Images, pictures and metaphors no longer seem to reach us. God (if he is there) no longer communicates with us through the senses. In more modern terms, it is a matter of living from a center other than the ego. Even to begin to do this is to enter a great darkness, a new kind of light or illumination comes; and through it our relationship to God, although more hidden than before, becomes deeper and more direct."[6]

This experience of darkness is integral to the spirituality of the *discipline of the secret*. With the ego purged and the heart purified through the trials of the dark night, the interior life of an authentic disciple is a hidden, invisible affair. Today it appears that God is calling many ordinary Christians into this rhythm of loss and gain. The hunger I encounter across the land for silence, solitude, and centering prayer is the Spirit of Christ calling us from the shallows to the deep.

Undoubtedly in each of our lives there were periods of intense fervor when we could almost touch the goodness of God. Bible studies, prayer meetings, retreats, and devotional time were precious securities to many of us. It was pleasant to think about God, a comfort to speak to Him, a joy to be in His presence. Perhaps all this has changed. We may feel we have lost Christ and fear that He will never return. Now it is difficult to connect two thoughts about Him. Prayer has become artificial. Words spoken to Him ring hollow in our empty soul. Worse, oppressive feelings of guilt sharpen the sense of loss. Night closes in around us. We have failed Him. It is all our fault.

It is a comfort to know that this is a path that many have tracked before us. Moreover it is reassuring to learn that the longed-for growth in faith is not far away. God's love and mercy have not abandoned us. Clouds may shroud us in darkness, but above the sun shines bright. God's mercy never fails. The Christian who surrenders in trust to this truth finds Jesus Christ in a new way. It marks the beginning of a deeper life of faith where joy and peace flourish *even in the darkness,* because they are rooted, not in superficial human feelings, but deep down in the dark certainty of faith that Jesus is the same, yesterday, today, and forever.

The very inability to feel His presence with our unstable emotions or to appreciate His goodness with our feeble thoughts becomes a help rather than a hindrance. Joy and sorrow may play havoc with our feelings, but beneath this shifting surface God dwells in the darkness. It is there that we go to meet Him; it is there that we pray in peace, silent and attentive to the God whose love knows no shadow of change. It is there that we *celebrate the darkness* in the quiet certainty of mature faith.

"The contemplative is not the man or woman who has fiery visions of the cherubim . . . but simply he who has risked his mind in the desert beyond language and beyond ideas where God is encountered in the nakedness of pure trust, that is to say, in the surrender of our poverty and incompleteness, in order no longer to clench our minds in a cramp upon themselves, as if thinking made us exist. The message the contemplative offers is not that you need to find your way through the language and problems that today surround God, but whether you understand or not, God loves us, is present to you, lives in you, dwells in you, calls you, saves you and offers you an understanding and light which are like nothing you have ever found in books or heard in sermons."[7]

The theology of the dark night is simplicity itself. God strips us of natural delights and spiritual consolations in order to enter more fully into our hearts. Christian maturity lies in allowing God the freedom to work His sovereign wisdom in us, neither abandoning a disciplined life of prayer in frustration nor running to the many distractions the busy world affords us. What comes to mind is the image of a branch plunged several times into fire. As the fire scorches the wood, it burns away all the natural saps and juices proper to the wood. At first, the wood is charred and ugly. Each time it is thrust into the fire, the purging process continues. Finally when all the natural juices that have been resisting the action of the fire are burnt away, the wood takes on the beautiful qualities of the fire itself and glows.

The graces of prayer, humility, detachment, and a deepened faith are the beautiful qualities of the flame. We can only obtain those qualities through the purging action of God's grace. In this purification process we are prepared to receive the gifts we have prayed for.

When we have hit bottom and are totally emptied of all we thought important to us, then we truly pray, truly become humble and detached, and live in the bright darkness of faith. In the midst of the emptying we know that God has not deserted us. He has merely removed the obstacles keeping us from a deeper union with Him. Actually we are closer to God than ever before, although we are deprived of the consolations that we once associated with our spirituality. What we thought was communion with Him was really a hindrance to that communion.

Yet the dark night is not the end—only the means to union with God. We have asked God for the gift of prayer and He visits us with adversity to bring us to our knees. We have prayed for humility and God levels us with humiliation. We cry out for an increase of faith and God strips us of the reassurances that we had identified with faith. Does growth in Christ follow automatically?

No. Suffering alone does not produce a prayerful spirit. Humiliation alone does not foster humility. Desolation alone does not guarantee the increase of faith. These experiences merely dispose us to prayer, humility, and faith. We can still be wallowing in self-pity and rebellion, wounded pride or stoic apathy and the last state will be worse than the first. We can eat humble pie until the bakery is bare, and emerge with only tightfisted bitterness in our hands. One further crucial step in the process of ego-slaying remains.

The most characteristic feature of the humility of Jesus is His *forgiveness and acceptance of others*. By contrast, our nonacceptance and lack of forgiveness keep us in a state of agitation and unrest. Our resentments reveal that the signature of Jesus is still not written on our lives. The surest sign of union with the crucified Christ is our forgiveness of those who have perpetrated injustices against us. Without acceptance and forgiveness the dark night will be only that. The bottom line will be a troubled heart. Forgiveness of enemies seals our participation in the dark night of Jesus Christ who cried out in behalf of His killers: "Forgive them, Father, they know not what they do."

One night years ago in the monastery in Steubenville, Ohio, a number of brothers were naming the greatest book each had ever read, excluding the Bible. One learned man said *The Confessions of St. Augustine* towered over all others. Another friar nominated the *Summa Theologica* of Thomas Aquinas. A third added *The Mystalogical Catechesis* of Cyril of Jerusalem. Without blinking an eye, I said the most powerful book other than Scripture that I have ever read is Hans Küng's *On Being a Christian*. For me no one has ever written or spoken with such passionate intelligence on the dark night of Jesus Christ. Here is a quote from this book:

"Jesus' unresisting suffering and helpless death, accursed and dishonored, for his enemies and even his friends, was the unmistakeable sign that he was finished and had nothing to do with the true God. His death on the cross was the fulfillment of the curse of the law. 'Anyone hanged on a tree is cursed by God.' He was wrong wholly and entirely: in his message, his behavior, his whole being. His claim is now refuted, his authority gone, his way shown to be false. . . . The heretical teacher is condemned, the false prophet disowned, the seducer of the people unmasked, the blasphemer rejected. The law had triumphed over this 'gospel.' . . .

"Jesus found himself left alone, not only by his people, but by the One to whom he had constantly appealed as no one did before him. Left absolutely alone. We do not know what Jesus thought and felt as he was dying. But it was obvious to the whole world that he had proclaimed the early advent of God in his kingdom and this God did not come. A God who was man's friend, knowing all his needs, close to him, but this God was absent. A Father whose goodness knew no bounds, providing for the slightest things and the humblest people, gracious and at the same time mighty; but this Father gave no sign, produced no miracles.

"His Father indeed, to whom he had spoken with a familiarity closer than anyone else had ever known, with whom he had lived and worked in a unity beyond the ordinary, whose true will he had learned with immediate certainty and in the light of which he had dared to assure individuals of the forgiveness of their sins; this Father of his did not say a single word. Jesus, God's witness, was left in the lurch by the God to whom he had witnessed. The mockery at the foot of the cross underlined vividly this wordless, helpless, miracle-less and even God-less death.

"The unique communion with God which he had seemed to enjoy only makes his forsakenness more unique. This God and Father with whom he had identified himself to the very end did not at the end identify himself with the sufferer. And so everything seemed as if it had never been: in vain. He who had announced the closeness and advent of God his Father publicly before the whole world died utterly forsaken by God and was thus publicly demonstrated as godless before the whole world: someone judged by God himself, disposed of once and for all. And since the cause for which he had lived and fought was so closely linked to his person, so that cause fell with his person. There was no cause independent of his person. How could anyone have believed his word after he had been silenced and died in this outrageous fashion? It is a death not simply accepted in patience but endured screaming to God. . . ."[8]

A graphic description of the dark night of Jesus Christ. No human mind will ever comprehend the depths of desolation, the indescribable loneliness, the utter abandonment that lay behind Jesus' cry, "Eloi, Eloi, lama sabachthani—My God, My God, why have You forsaken Me?" The cross is both the symbol of our salvation and the pattern of our lives. Everything that happened to Christ in some way happens to us. When darkness envelops us and we are deaf to everything except the shriek of our own pain, it helps to know that the Father is tracing in us the image of His Son, that the signature of Jesus is being stamped on our souls.

For Jesus the darkness of night gave way to the light of morning. "God highly exalted Him, and bestowed on Him the name which is above every name, that at the name of Jesus every knee should bow, of those who are in heaven, and on earth, and under the earth, and that every tongue should confess that Jesus Christ is Lord, to the glory of God the Father" (Philippians 2:9–11, NAS).

Forgiveness is the key to everything. It forms the mind of Christ within us and prevents the costly and painful process of the dark night from itself becoming an ego trip. It guards us from feeling so "spiritually advanced" that we look down on those who are still enjoying the comforts and consolations of the first conversion. The "gentle and humble in heart" have the mind of Christ.

Henri Nouwen tells the story of an old man who used to meditate early every morning under a big tree on the bank of the Ganges river. One morning, after he had finished his meditation, the old man opened his eyes and saw a scorpion floating helplessly in the water. As the scorpion was washed closer to the tree, the old man quickly stretched himself out on one of the long roots that branched out into the river and reached out to rescue the drowning creature. As soon as he touched it, the scorpion stung him. Instinctively the man withdrew his hand. A minute later, after he had regained his balance, he stretched himself out again on the roots to save the scorpion. This time the scorpion stung him so badly with its poisonous tail that his hand became swollen and bloody and his face contorted with pain.

At that moment, a passerby saw the old man stretched out on the roots struggling with the scorpion and shouted: "Hey, stupid old man, what's wrong with you? Only a fool would risk his life for the sake of an ugly, evil creature. Don't you know you could kill yourself trying to save that ungrateful scorpion?"

The old man turned his head. Looking into the stranger's eyes he said calmly, "My friend, just because it is the scorpion's nature to sting, that does not change my nature to save."

Sitting here at the typewriter in my study, I turn to the symbol of the crucified Christ on the wall to my left. And I hear Jesus praying for His murderers, "Father, forgive them. They do not know what they are doing."

The scorpion He had tried to save finally killed Him. To me, the passerby, who sees Him stretched out on the tree roots and who shouts, "Only a madman would risk his life for the sake of an ugly, ungrateful creature," Jesus answers, "My friend, just because it is fallen mankind's nature to wound, that does not change My nature to save."

Here is the final repudiation of the ego. We surrender the need for vindication, hand over the kingdom of self to the Father, and in the sovereign freedom of forgiving our enemies, celebrate the luminous darkness.

Seven

The
Love of Jesus

Down the corridor of time Christians have attempted to cope in various ways with the overwhelming reality of the person of Jesus Christ. I define *coping* as "our personal response of adaptation or adjustment produced by the encounter with the real Jesus."

There is a tendency in every Christian mind to remake the Man of Galilee, to concoct the kind of Jesus we can live with, to project a Christ who confirms our preferences and prejudices. The great English poet John Milton, for example, framed an intellectual Christ who scorned common people as "a herd confused, a miscellaneous rabble who extol things vulgar."

The tendency to construct a Christ in our own terms of reference and to reject any evidence that challenges our life situations and assumptions is human and universal.

For many hippies in the '60s, Jesus was much like them-selves—an agitator and social critic, a dropout from the ratrace, a prophet of the counterculture. For many yup-pies in the '80s, Jesus is the provider of the good life, the Lord of the spa, a driven young executive with a messianic mission, the prophet of prosperity and the chauffered limousine. After all, didn't He promise us a hundredfold in this life?

Is either the hippie Jesus or the yuppie Jesus a faithful portrait of the courageous, dynamic, free, and demanding Jesus of the New Testament?

In the delightful musical *Godspell* we are presented with a sunshine gospel where carnival innocence, marvelous humor, and youthful energy sing a lullaby to the soul and entice us into a world of no personal accountability. Its selective approach gives a rollicking but essentially false idea of the Gospel message. The crucifixion is an embar-rassing "theological necessity" to be hastily hurdled. The resurrection is reduced to a song, "Long Live God." What do we make of a gospel without the paschal mystery? Where is the signature of Jesus?

In Malachi Martin's book *Jesus Now,* the author surveys the historical distortions of Jesus through the ages. First there is "Jesus Caesar." In his name the Church combined wealth and political power with professed service to God, an unsacramental marriage of Church and state where the Pope in his ermine cape and Caesar in silk toga banded together to build empires. We find the same unholy alliance in our nation's capital today as certain religious leaders stalk the corridors of power baptizing some poli-ticians and blacklisting others, always claiming to find support in the teaching of Jesus.

"Jesus Apollo" came later: a romantic visionary, a beautiful human leader with no disturbing overtones. He became the hero of the charming and gifted gentlemen of the nineteenth and early twentieth centuries, thinkers like

121

Thoreau and Ralph Waldo Emerson. But Jesus Apollo never dirtied his hands, never walked into a migrant worker camp in Miami or a slum in New York City. He was no Savior. He did not advocate a living wage, decent housing, civil rights, or care for the aged.

In every age and culture we tend to shape Jesus to our own image and make Him over to our own needs in order to cope with the stress His unedited presence creates. "In a foxhole Jesus is a rescue squad; in a dentist's chair a painkiller; on exam day a problem-solver; in an affluent society a clean-shaven middle-of-the-roader; for a Central American guerilla a bearded revolutionary."[1] If we think of Jesus as the friend of sinners, the sinners are likely to be our kind of people. I know, for instance, that Jesus befriends alcoholics. My personal history and cultural conditioning make Jesus congenial and compassionate with selective sinners just like myself. I can cope with this Jesus.

Blaise Pascal wrote: "God made man in his own image and man returned the compliment." Through five decades I have seen Christians shaping Jesus in their own image—in each case a dreadfully small deity. In his classic work *Your God Is Too Small*, J. B. Phillips enumerated several of the caricatures: Resident Policeman, Parental Hangover, Grand Old Man, Meek-and-Mild, Heavenly Bosom, Managing Director, God in a Hurry, God for the Elite, God without Godhead, etc.

The same tendency persists today in Christology, especially in the disciples of "Jesus Torquemada." In the fifteenth century they persecuted and tortured anyone who dared to disagree with their limited interpretation of Scripture. Torquemada, whose Spanish name means "orthodoxy of doctrine," died an old man in 1498, responsible for two thousand burnings at the stake and the exiling of 160,000 Jews from Spain as undesirable aliens—all for the glory of God. Torquemadeans are alive and well today in every Christian denomination and non-denomination. The same meanmindedness, jealousy, ostracism, and hatred still divide the Body of Christ.

In reply to His haunting question "Who do you say that I am?" my own experience of Jesus Christ cries out: "You are the Son of God, the revealer of the Father's love." This astonishing truth, that Jesus embodies for us a Father who loves us even when we fail to love, is the Good News. The revelation that we are loved in an incomparable way empowers us to be fools for Christ, to embrace the *discipline of the secret,* to celebrate the darkness under the signature of Jesus. "For Christ's love compels us" (2 Corinthians 5:14, NIV).

However, my past twenty-five years of pastoral experience indicate that the stunning disclosure that God is love has had negligible impact on the majority of Christians and minimal transforming power. The problem seems to be: either we don't know it or know it but cannot accept it; or we accept it but are not in touch with it; or we are in touch with it but do not surrender to it.

In spite of our reluctance and resistance, the essence and novelty of the New Covenant is that the very law of God's being is love. Pagan philosophers like Plato and Aristotle had arrived through human reasoning at the existence of God, speaking of Him in vague, impersonal terms as the Uncaused Cause and the Immovable Mover. The prophets of Israel had revealed the God of Abraham, Isaac, and Jacob in a more intimate and passionate manner. But only Jesus revealed that God is a Father of incomparable tenderness, that if we take all the goodness, wisdom, and compassion of the best mothers and fathers who have ever lived, they would only be a faint shadow of the love and mercy in the heart of the redeeming God.

Christianity moves in a climate completely penetrated by love and we are called to a life of discipleship compatible with it, not living at a pre-Christian level eyeing God solely in terms of laws, rules, and obligations. God is love. We are called by Jesus Christ into an intimate friendship in which one member is a human being and the other the eternal God. We are invited to personal dialogue with the Holy One who is unreservedly involved with us. In His own Person Jesus radically affirmed that God is not indifferent to human suffering. Jesus is God's Word to the world saying, "See how I love you."

If anyone should ask you, "What is the one thing in life that is certain?" before saying, "Death and taxes," a disciple must answer, "The love of Christ." Not parents, not friends—even the finest and dearest; not art, science, philosophy, or any of the products of human wisdom. Only the love of Jesus Christ made manifest on the cross is certain. We cannot even say, "God's love," because the truth that God is love we know ultimately only through the signature of Jesus.

Over a hundred years ago in the deep South, a phrase commonplace in our Christian culture today, *born again*, was seldom used. Rather, the words used to describe the breakthrough into a personal relationship with Jesus Christ were: "I was seized by the power of a great affection."

It was a profoundly moving way to indicate both the initiative of almighty God and the explosion within the human heart when Jesus becomes Lord. Seized by the power of a great affection was a visceral description of the phenomenon of Pentecost, authentic conversion, and the release of the Holy Spirit.

In March 1986 I was privileged to spend an afternoon with an Amish family in Lancaster, Pennsylvania. Jonas Zook, a widower, is eighty-two years old. His oldest daughter Barbara, 57, manages the household. The three younger children, Rachel, 53, Elam, 47, and Sam, 45, are all severely retarded. When I arrived at noon with two friends, Joe and Kathy Anders, "little Elam"—about four feet tall, heavy-set, thickly bearded, and wearing the black Amish outfit with the circular hat—was coming out of the barn some fifty yards away. He had never laid eyes on me in his life, yet when he saw me step out of the car, this little Mongoloid ran lickety-split in my direction. Two feet away, he threw himself into the air, wrapped his arms around my neck, his legs around my waist, and kissed me on the lips with fierce intensity for a full thirty seconds.

To say that I was stunned would be an understatement. But in the twinkling of an eye, Jesus set me free. I buried my lips into Elam's and returned his kiss with the same enthusiasm. Then he jumped down, wrapped both his hands around my right arm, and led me on a tour of the farm. The Zooks raised piglets for a living.

A half hour later, at a lovely luncheon prepared by Barbara, Elam sat next to me. Midway through the meal, I turned 'round to say something to Joe Anders. Inadvertently, my right elbow slammed into Elam's rib cage. He did not wince; he did not groan. He wept like a two-year-old child. His next move utterly undid me. Elam came over to my chair, planted himself on my lap, and kissed me even harder on the lips. Then he kissed my eyes, my nose, my forehead, and cheeks. And there was Brennan, dazed, dumbstruck, weeping, seized by the power of a great affection. In his simplicity, little Elam Zook was an icon of Jesus Christ. Why? Because his love for me did not stem from any attractiveness or lovability of mine. It was not conditioned by any response on my part. Elam loved me whether I was kind or unkind, pleasant or nasty. His love arose from a source outside of himself and myself.

It brought to mind something I had read years ago in a book on native Americans. The Iroquois Indians attributed divinity to retarded children, gave them a place of honor in the tribe, and treated them as gods. In their unselfconsciousness they were a transparent window into the Great Spirit, into the heart of Jesus who loves us as we are and not as we should be, beyond worthiness and unworthiness, beyond fidelity and infidelity, who loves us in the morning sun and the evening rain without caution, regret, boundary, limit, or breaking point.

Jesus came as revealer of the nature of the Godhead, as the revealer of love. To paraphrase John's prologue: When all things began, the Word already was. The Word dwelt with God, and what God was, the Word was. In other words, if one looked at Jesus one saw God, for "he who has seen Me has seen the Father" (John 14:9, NAS). Jesus is the complete expression of God. Through Him as through no one else God spoke and acted. When one met Him one was met and judged and saved by God. This is what the apostles bore witness to. In this man, in His life, death, and resurrection they had experienced God at work.

For "God was in Christ reconciling the world to Himself" (2 Corinthians 5:19, NAS). God vested himself utterly and completely in the Man Jesus of Nazareth. In Him all His fullness dwells. What God is, Christ is. "He who believes in Me, does not believe in Me, but in Him who sent Me" (John 12:44, NAS). Jesus reveals God by being utterly transparent to Him. What had been cloaked in mystery is clear in Jesus—that God is love. No man or woman has ever loved like Jesus Christ. Therein lies His divinity for me.

At some point in His human journey Jesus was seized by the power of a great affection and experienced the love of His Father in a way that burst all previous boundaries of understanding. It may have happened during His hidden years in Nazareth (sometime between the ages of twenty and thirty before He began his public ministry). Throughout the equivalent of His high school and college and post-graduate years, Jesus prayerfully ponders His relationship with His Father. Finally the day arrives when Jesus announces to His mother that He has to leave Nazareth. The intimacy of trust and love for God has become decisive enough to call Jesus away from home. He must follow His own inner light and be where the Father is for Him.

At about age thirty Jesus sets out for the River Jordan to meet with the Baptist. John is bluntly calling the Jewish community to repentance and arousing the first stirrings of conversion. Jesus gets in line. His behavior reveals the sense of identity and mission that has been growing within Him. John reluctantly confers baptism and Jesus identifies with the brotherhood of sin. "He made Him who knew no sin to be sin on our behalf" (2 Corinthians 5:21, NAS).

Then it happens! Whatever the external manifestations were, the baptism of Jesus Christ in the River Jordan was an awesome personal experience. The heavens are split, the Spirit descends in the form of a dove, and Jesus hears the words, "You are My Son, My Beloved, on you My favor rests." What an earthquake in the human soul of Jesus! The heavenly voice confirms and fulfills thirty years of search and growth in Nazareth. It ratifies His reply to His mother in the Temple at age twelve: "Didn't you know I must always be where My Father is?" In this decisive experience at the Jordan Jesus learns that He is Son-Servant-Beloved of His Father.

From this moment Jesus is wrapped in the aloneness of a lover with his beloved. His life is one of deepening intimacy with His Father. His feet and eyes will continue their human search but the Breath of the Father is on His face. Now He is driven by the Spirit into the wilderness.

He sits on rocks under the hot sun and walks the barren desert listening to the sounds of silence. Slowly, the word that He heard as John baptized Him, the word that was the most extraordinary religious experience of His life, lays hold of Him with great and growing power—the Word of his own *belovedness*.[2] He hears the words "beloved Son" whispered to Him over and over again in his deepest consciousness. The Father is speaking directly and personally to Him with words of tender love and an indication of some special destiny. His response, rising from the depths of His soul, is *Abba*—a term more intimate than *Father*, which after that day is ever at the heart of His prayer.

In the chastening solitude of that uncluttered wilderness Jesus is seized by the power of a great affection. The Father speaks the word that confirms Jesus as the Christ and thus alters the direction of human history. "You are My dear, beloved Son," a clear, core identity experience filling Jesus with a profound sense of His person and His mission.

Let us not hurry past this moment in search of "deeper" revelations of Jesus. The Abba experience is the source and secret of His being, His message, and manner of life. It can only be appreciated by those who share it. Until we meet the Abba of Jesus ourselves and experience Him to be a loving, forgiving Daddy, it is virtually impossible to understand Jesus' teaching on love. Jesus' awareness of His own belovedness fills Him with awe:

"God loves Me. I am a humble carpenter from Nazareth and yet God loves Me. In the scorching heat and aching loneliness of this wilderness I can feel it. I am the beloved Son of the center of the universe. The Creator God is Abba, a Daddy to Me, a loving Father in whose sight I am precious. I am welcome in My Father's house. Everyone is welcome. That's it! Everyone is welcome. I must go and tell My brothers and sisters that they are dear children of the Most High God. . . . The Pharisees are all wrong. They have made religion so complex, so legalistic and rigid. The people are full of fear. I must go and set them free."[3]

I realize that this is an imaginative reconstruction of what happened in the developing consciousness of Jesus. Nothing written here, however, is inconsistent with the

Gospel evidence. Were there human limitations in Him whom we call Lord? Relying on sound biblical and theological scholarship I deeply affirm that Jesus subjected Himself to the limits of humanity and fully embraced the human condition. Without in any way denying the divine eternal sonship of Jesus as revelation sent from the Father and strongly affirming the statement of the Council of Nicea that Jesus is "true God and true man," I accept a developing consciousness in Christ both as to His person and His mission. Such acceptance does nothing to detract from the dignity of Jesus. Rather, acknowledging the human limitations of Jesus helps us to better understand what Paul meant when he wrote to the Philippians, "He emptied Himself," and to a deeper appreciation that God loved us so much that He subjected Himself to all our infirmities. Accepting the limitations of Jesus' knowledge reveals to what depths divine condescension went in the incarnation. It shows how human was the humanity of Jesus.

The early Church father Cyril of Jerusalem wrote of Christ: "We have admired his goodness in that for love of us he has not refused to descend to such a low position as to bear all that belongs to our nature, included in which is *ignorance*."[4]

In order to understand the relentless tenderness and passionate love of Jesus Christ we must always return to His Abba experience. He experienced God as tender and loving, courteous and kind, compassionate and forgiving, as Laughter of the Morning and Comfort of the Night. Abba, a colloquial form of address used by little Jewish children toward their fathers and best translated Papa or Daddy, opened up the possibility of undreamed-of, unheard-of intimacy with God. In any other great world religion it is unthinkable to address almighty God as Abba. "Many devout Moslems, Buddhists and Hinduists are generous and sincere in their search for God. Many have had profound mystical experiences. Yet in spite of their immeasurable spiritual depth, they seldom or never come to know God as their Father. Indeed, intimacy with Abba is one of the greatest treasures Jesus has brought us."[5]

Nor, according to Joachim Jeremias, does "Abba" have any parallel in Hebrew literature—prophetic, apocalyptic, or any other kind. Jesus alone knew God as Daddy. "No one knows the Father except the Son and those to whom the Son chooses to reveal Him."

Abba—the overtones of this small word will always escape us. Yet in it we sense the intense intimacy of Jesus with His Father. We touch the heart of His faith. We come to understand the mind of Christ. The Abba relationship made Him the Person He was. It freed Him from the limited religious understanding of His time and enabled Him to relate to prostitutes and Pharisees, sinners and Sadducees with warmth, ease, openness, and liberating love.

The parables of divine mercy—the lost coin, the lost sheep, and the lost son—are rooted in Jesus' own experience of His Abba. He speaks wholly and entirely in the light of this reality. These stories were intended not only to defend His notorious conduct with sinners, but to startle His critics by cracking through their conventional ways of thinking about God. Jesus skewered His opponents with words to this effect: "The harlots who have no imagined righteousness to protect will be dancing into the Kingdom while you have your alleged virtue burnt out of you! Hear me well: I have come to announce the dawn of a new age, an era of incredible generosity. Allow yourselves to be captivated by joy and wonder at the surpassing greatness of My Father's love for the lost; set it over against your own joyless, loveless, thankless, and self-righteous lives. Let go of your impoverished understanding of God and your circumscribed notion of morality.

Cease from your loveless ways. Celebrate the homecoming of the lost and rejoice in My Father's munificence."

The proclamation of the Kingdom was born from the urgency in the heart of Jesus. It was crucial that He bring the Good News of the Gospel of grace: If only people could realize their own *belovedness*, their lives would be transformed and a new Kingdom would spring into being.

You and I are not only invited but actually called to enter into this warm and liberating experience of God as Abba. In Romans 8, Paul is explicit: "You have not received a spirit of slavery leading to fear again, but you have received a spirit of adoption as sons by which we cry out, 'Abba, Father!' " (Romans 8:15, NAS). We are privileged to share in the intimacy of Jesus with His Father. We are called to live and to celebrate the same freedom that made Jesus so attractive and authentic.

Recently a 27-year-old recovering alcoholic came to me for counseling. He had been born and raised a Roman Catholic but hadn't worked at it. He had been married six times. His life was a tragic story of waste and wandering, boozing and womanizing. He asked me to help him return to the Church. Normally my first reaction would have been to assure him that Jesus welcomed home the lost sheep and then pass quickly into outlining the canonical process of getting his first marriage annulled on the grounds of emotional and spiritual immaturity, whereupon all his other marriages would also be canonically invalid. I would have urged him to confess his sins, to have his first marriage annulled in the internal forum of the sacrament of reconciliation, and afterward to go to Mass and receive Communion.

But I found that the old tapes weren't spinning around in my head. I wasn't replaying the dry-souled juridical office of the "pastoral counselor." I looked beyond the technical problem the man had brought to me. What I saw was a 27-year-old kid, a child of the Father whose soiled life was filled with squalid choices and failed dreams. Alcoholism had torn his life apart, unraveled the fabric of any moral training he might have received. He was broken, alienated from himself and God, a stranger in a strange land.

Then, like a peal of rolling thunder in the distance, I got in touch with the unspeakable anguish, the convulsive torment, the utter desolation that would be mine if Roslyn ever said she didn't like me anymore, that she didn't want to live with me, that she wanted a divorce. This kid's life, spent mostly in an alcoholic fog, had been shredded six times. Tears were rolling down my face. I reached out, embraced him, held him for a long time, and said, "I have a word for you from your brother Jesus: Welcome home." He was sobbing and asked, "Tell me who Jesus is." I told him about my own tarnished past and the Jesus I had met in my need. We prayed. He accepted Jesus as his Savior. Light broke into his darkness. Peace filled our hearts.

Later when I was alone, the specter of canonical irregularity rose before me and I felt a twinge of guilt for not observing due process. A quiet calm came when I prayed, "Dear Jesus, if it's a fault for being too kind to a sinner, then it's a fault I learned from You. For You never scolded anyone or brandished the Law at anyone who came to You seeking understanding and mercy."

Further along in His ministry, Jesus would say: "The Father and I are one," indicating an intimacy of life and love that defy description. To Philip He would say, "He who sees Me sees the Father." And again, "It is the Father living in Me who is doing this work." Jesus is the human face of God, with all the attitudes, attributes, and characteristics of the Father.

So many Christians I know stop at Jesus. They remain on the Way without going where the Way leads them—to the Father. They want to be brothers and sisters without being sons and daughters. In them, the lament of Jesus in John 17 is fulfilled: "Father, Righteous One, the world has not known you" (verse 25, JB).

The Abba experience fired Jesus with a towering zeal to proclaim the Good News of the Kingdom—a Kingdom of compassion, love, and forgiveness. As the Father loved Him, so Jesus would love us and invite us to do the same. "Love one another as I have loved you."

Jesus challenges us to forgive everyone we know and even those we don't know and to be very careful not to forget even one against whom we harbor ill will. Right now someone exists who has disappointed and offended us, someone with whom we are continually displeased and with whom we are more impatient, irritated, unforgiving, and spiteful than we would dare be with anyone else. That person is ourselves. We are so often fed up with ourselves. We're sick of our own mediocrity, revolted by our own inconsistency, bored by our own monotony. We would never judge any other of God's children with the savage self-condemnation with which we crush ourselves. Jesus said we are to love our neighbor as ourselves. We must be patient, gentle, and compassionate with ourselves in the same way we try to love our neighbor. I must be with Brennan what I was with the 27-year-old recovering alcoholic.

Through an intimate, heartfelt knowledge of Jesus Christ we learn to forgive ourselves. To the extent that we allow His kindness, patience, and incredible trust toward us to win us over, we'll be freed from that dislike of ourselves that follows us everywhere. It is simply not possible to know the love of Jesus for us unless we alter our opinions and feelings about ourselves, and side with Him in His all-accepting love for us. Christ's forgiveness reconciles us with Him, with ourselves, and with the whole community. According to Bernard Bush, one way to know how Jesus feels about you is: If you love yourself intensely and freely, then your feelings about yourself correspond perfectly to the sentiments of Jesus.

Jesus' intimacy with Abba God is translated into an intimate relationship with His disciples. He draws near to us and speaks in words of intense familiarity. "My little children, I shall not be with you much longer. . . . I will not leave you orphans. I will come back to you. I am going to prepare a place for you. I shall return to take you with Me." The Jesus who speaks here is not just a teacher or a model for us to imitate. He offers Himself to each of us as companion for the journey, as a friend who is patient with us, kind, never rude, quick to forgive, and whose love keeps no score of wrongs. This is a beautiful dimension of discipleship, and the New Testament lays great stress on it:

"Here I stand, knocking at the door. If anyone hears Me calling and opens the door, I will enter his house, and dine with him. . . . Anyone who loves Me will be true to My Word, and My Father will love him: and We will come to him and make our dwelling place with him. . . . And know that I am with you always, even till the end of the world. . . . No longer do I call you servants; I have called you friends."

St. Augustine's commentary on this last verse was: "A friend is someone who knows everything about you and still accepts you." This is the dream we all share: that one day I may meet the person to whom I can really talk, who will understand me and the words I say, and even hear what is left unsaid—and still will go on liking me.[6] Jesus Christ is the fulfillment of this dream.

In a recent newsletter I wrote: "A friend is someone who stays with you in the bad weather of life, guards you when you are off your guard, restrains your impetuosity, delights in your presence, forgives your failures, does not forsake you when others let you down, and shares whatever he or she might be having for breakfast (as Jesus did on the beach along the Sea of Tiberias)—fish and chips, moon pie, cold pizza, or chocolate cake and milk." As the old hymn reminds us: What a friend we have in Jesus! A reality that dizzies the mind and dazzles the imagination! The beloved Son of the Father wants us to know, to realize and experience our own *belovedness*. "As the Father has loved Me, so have I loved you."

Is this sense of belovedness real to you? Has it become jaded through repetition? Or, like a knife slashing through wallpaper, has it led to a dramatic breakthrough into intimacy with God? A couple of weeks ago in San Jose, California, a woman of about thirty-five came up to me and said, "We've never met, but I want you to know that the sentence at the top of page eighty in your book *A Stranger to Self-Hatred* changed my life." When I asked her what the sentence was, she quoted from memory: "Jesus loves us as we are and not as we should be, since none of us is as we should be."

The life of Paul is anchored in his intimate friendship with Jesus. "Life to me, of course, is Christ" (Philippians 1:21, JB). Daily Paul turns his life over to Jesus, trusts Him, praises Him, asks Him for what he needs, finds his *raison d'etre* in Him, and gratefully receives His love, which knows no shadow of change. He "loved me, and delivered Himself up for me" (Galatians 2:20, NAS). Never let these words be interpreted as mere intellectualizing by Paul. The love of Jesus Christ was a burning and divine reality for him, and his life is utterly incomprehensible except in terms of it. Paul would have been buried in history as an unknown zealot except for his immense, uncompromising love for the person of Jesus. If you approached Paul and wanted to discuss parish renewal or contemporary worship, he would answer, "I have no understanding of church or religion except in terms of the sacred man Jesus who loved me and delivered Himself up for me." Paul uses the phrase *in Christ* 164 times in his letters to describe what discipleship is all about. He is a powerful witness to the connectedness Jesus described in His farewell discourse: "I am the vine, you are the branches. The person who lives in Me and I in him will produce abundantly, for apart from Me you can do nothing."

The vine is the most intimate of all plants, growing over

itself, into and around itself, intricately connected with all its parts. Jesus' image "I am the vine" is the perfect expression of intimacy.

The late Tony DeMello told a story illustrating the warm familiarity of friendship with Christ. A priest went to visit a terminally ill man in his home. As he entered the bedroom, he noticed a chair at the man's bedside and asked him what it was doing there. The sick man replied, "I had placed Jesus on that chair and was talking to Him before you arrived. For years," he continued, "I found it extremely difficult to pray until a friend explained to me that prayer was simply a matter of talking with Jesus. He told me to place an empty chair nearby, to imagine Jesus sitting on that chair, and to speak with Him and listen to what He says to me in reply. I've had no difficulty in praying ever since."

Some days later the daughter of the sick man came to the parish house to inform the priest that her father had just died. She said, "I left him alone for a couple of hours. He seemed so peaceful. When I got back to the room, I found him dead. I noticed a strange thing, though: His head was resting not on the bed but on an empty chair that was beside his bed."[7]

The paternal love of Abba is revealed as fraternal love in our brother Jesus. What depths of intimacy we are invited to! "As the Father has loved Me, so I have loved you." Prayer is simply relaxing and delighting in Jesus with no agenda except celebrating the deep affection between you. This interpersonal encounter deepens the sense of our own belovedness and alters our relationships with others.

Jesus deepens human friendship as He deepens everything He touches. Without Him, we find it difficult to relate to some people in a loving and respectful way. A certain stiffness coupled with a critical attitude prevent us from offering what they need most—encouragement for their lives. We restrict our warmth and acceptance to a selected few. The friendship of Jesus enables us to see others as He saw the Twelve, flawed but good, wounded healers, children of the Father. We discover that we are compatible with a wide spectrum of people with whom we used to be uncomfortable and begin to pray, as Thomas Merton did, "I thank You, God, that I am like the rest of men."

I am now writing these words in a chilly, dimly lit cabin tucked away in the Santa Cruz Mountains of northern California. If you picture to yourself the letter V, my cabin is right at the bottom of the valley where the diagonal lines converge—the lines represent the mountains that tower on both sides. I've been here for six days in silence and solitude. This retreat has been a journey from absurdity to obedience. *Absurd* comes from the Latin *surdus* meaning "deaf." *Obedience* comes from the Latin *ob audire* meaning "to listen to." Our busy world too often makes us deaf to the voice of God who speaks to us in silence.

Thus it is not surprising that we often wonder, in the midst of our occupied and preoccupied lives, if anything is really happening. Our lives may be filled to overflowing— so many events and commitments that we wonder how we'll get it all done. Yet, at the same time, we might feel unfulfilled and wonder if anything is worth living for. Being filled yet unfulfilled, busy yet bored, involved yet lonely, these are the symptoms of the absurd lifestyle that makes us inattentive to spiritual realities.

I came here to listen to the Voice whispering in nature, in Word and sacrament, in the people who have crossed my path and touched my life. Today I wandered along a nature trail through a dense redwood forest humming aloud, "When through the woods and forests glades I wander. . . ." I have a vivid image of myself staring up at 150-foot redwoods in utter stillness feeling tiny and insignificant and whispering, "How great Thou art! O Abba, who is man that You should be mindful of him?"

I have a sad confession to make: Until this week I have never been able to experience God in natural beauty. Something undeveloped or broken inside of me, or perhaps trapped subconsciously in a mindset that says only useful things count and superfluous things like redwoods and roses are unimportant, has rendered me insensitive to finding God in nature. However, the love of a little Pomeranian puppy named Binky-Boo, whom I reluctantly allowed into our home for the sake of our daughter Nicole, has opened me up to discovering God's presence in creation and finding with Shakespeare "tongues in trees, books in running brooks, sermons in stones and good in everything."

At night I have been staring shivering up at the stars. There is a freshness about finding the Milky Way when you haven't seen it for a while. The stars call us out of ourselves. During this retreat I have read the Gospel of John and eight of Paul's letters. In my journal I have jotted down different passages like: "No one has ever seen God; it is the only Son who is nearest to the Father's heart who has made Him known," and "God loved us with so much love that He was generous with His mercy; when we were dead through our sins, He brought us to life with Christ."

This is my last night in the cabin. I have prayed over John 21:15–17. Three times Jesus asks Peter, "Do you love Me?" Instantly I identified with Peter for my life has been the story of an unfaithful man through whom God continues to work. This is a word of consolation and liberation for me and anyone caught up in the oppression that Jesus works only through the 100-percenters, that discipleship must be an untarnished success story. It is a word of healing for those of us who have painfully discovered that we are earthen vessels in whom Jesus' prophecy to Peter has been fulfilled: "I tell you solemnly, this day, this night before the cock crows twice, you will have disowned Me three times."

I completed the prayer time, packed my suitcase, turned toward the door, and suddenly in faith I saw the risen Jesus with the holes, the wounds of love, in His hands and feet and side. I wept aloud. His warmth and affection came crashing down. It was overwhelming. I knew that I have not begun to know. Everything I have ever written, spoken, or experienced of the love of Jesus Christ is barely a hint, straw, dry leaves blowing in the wind.

In faith I heard Him say: "Three times I have asked, 'Do you love me?' Now face your shadow. Look carefully at what you most despise in yourself and then look through it. At your center you will discover a love for Me beyond words, images, and concepts, a love you are unable to understand or contain. Your love for me is fragile but real. Trust it."

It is only this wounded Jesus who provides the final revelation of God's love. The crucified Christ is not an abstraction but the ultimate answer to how far love will go, what measure of rejection it will endure, how much selfishness and betrayal it will withstand. The unconditional love of Jesus Christ nailed to the wood does not flinch before our perversity. "He took our sicknesses away and carried our diseases for us" (Matthew 8:17, JB).

In 1960, a pastor in East Germany wrote a play called *The Sign of Jonah*. The last scene dealt with the Final Judgment. All the peoples of the earth are assembled on the plain of Jehoshaphat awaiting God's verdict. They are not, however, waiting submissively; on the contrary they are gathered in small groups, talking indignantly. One group is a band of Jews, a sect that has known little but religious, social, and political persecution throughout their history. Included in their number are victims of Nazi extermination camps. Huddled together, the group demands to know what right God has to pass judgment on them, especially a God who dwells eternally in the security of heaven.

Another group consists of American blacks. They too question the authority of God who has never experienced the misfortunes of men, never known the squalor and depths of human degradation to which they were subjected in the suffocating holds of slave ships. A third group is composed of persons born illegitimately, the butt all their lives of jokes and sneers.

Hundreds of such groups are scattered across the plain: the poor, the afflicted, the maltreated. Each group appoints a representative to stand before the throne of God and challenge His divine right to pass sentence on their immortal destinies. The representatives include a horribly twisted arthritic, a victim of Hiroshima, a blind mute. They meet in council and decide that this remote and distant God who has never experienced human agony is unqualified to sit in judgment unless He is willing to enter into the suffering, humiliated state of man and endure what they have undergone.

Their conclusion reads: You must be born a Jew; the circumstances of your birth must be questioned; you must be misunderstood by everyone, insulted and mocked by your enemies, betrayed by your friends; you must be persecuted, beaten, and finally murdered in a most public and humiliating fashion.

Such is the judgment passed on God by the assembly. The clamor rises to fever pitch as they await His response. Then a brilliant, dazzling light illuminates the entire plain. One by one those who have passed judgment on God fall silent. For emblazoned high in the heavens for the whole world to see is the signature of Jesus Christ with this inscription above it: *I have served My sentence.*

Eight

The Dimensions of the Dragnet

"Jesus said he had never been to a football game. So we took him to one, my friends and I. It was a ferocious battle between the Protestant Punchers and the Catholic Crusaders.

"The Crusaders scored first. Jesus cheered wildly and threw his hat high up in the air. Then the Punchers scored. And Jesus cheered wildly and threw his hat high up in the air.

"This seemed to puzzle the man behind us. He tapped Jesus on the shoulder and asked, 'Which side are you rooting for, my good man?'

"'Me?' replied Jesus, by now visibly excited by the game. "Oh, I'm not rooting for either side. I'm just here to enjoy the game.'

"The questioner turned to his neighbor and sneered, 'Hmm, an atheist.'

"On the way back we briefed Jesus on the religious situation in the world today. 'It's a funny thing about religious people, Lord,' we said. 'They always seem to think that God is on their side and against the people on the other side.'

"Jesus agreed. 'That is why I don't back religions, I back people,' he said. 'People are more important than religions. Man is more important than the Sabbath.'

" 'You ought to watch your words,' one of us said with some concern. 'You were crucified once for saying that sort of thing, you know.'

" 'Yes, and by religious people,' said Jesus with a wry smile."[1]

Today all of us are guilty of the division in the Body of Christ. "May they all be one," Jesus prayed on the last night of His earthly life. "Father, may they be one in us, as you are in me and I am in you, so that the world may believe it was you who sent me. I have given them the glory you gave to me, that they may be one as we are one. With me in them and you in me, may they be so completely one that the world will realize that it was you who sent me" (John 17:21–23, JB). What an unbelieving world finds unbelievable is how different Christian communities, all claiming to love Christ, can be so scandalously at odds, can ignore, despise, and mistrust one another.

Almost 2,000 years after the birth of Christ we are divided by doctrine, history, and daily experience. "In doctrine we are still far apart. The words themselves are slender creatures: church and Bible, sin and grace, faith and works, pope and priest, revelation and tradition. But these slender syllables paint pictures, conjure up whole ways of life, suggest different understandings of the Christ-event, conflicting ideas of salvation, clashing answers to the question: how are God and man made one in Christ?

"Centuries of history sever us: every inquisition or forced conversion; every church burned or monastery sacked; each war of religion or legal restriction; each rack or rope; each worldly pope or Protestant prince; every cry of heresy or accusation of idolatry. . . .

"And we are divorced in day-to-day living: by parochial school and public school; by taxes and tax exemptions; by Catholic ghettoes and Protestant missions; by intolerant priests and bigoted ministers; by St. Patrick's Day and Reformation Day; . . . by the daily distrust and inherited fear—all the suspicion and dislike and hatred so often mingled with a mother's milk."[2]

What makes Christ credible is His love that knows no boundaries, frontiers, or sectarian divisions. And love alone makes Christianity credible. It is an observable fact that the *ekklesia* of Jesus Christ is least attractive when love is least evident. Scabrous stories about Christian disunity and "holy wars" are featured in *Time* and *Newsweek*. God and His Christ are not recognizable in us as Christian communities because we have denied the world the sole witness that makes the Gospel believable: "By this all men will know that you are My disciples, if you love one another." We have not lived the prayer of Jesus that we all might be one as He and the Father are one.

Authentic discipleship calls us to think, speak, and live the truth enunciated by Paul: "There is one body and one Spirit, one Lord, one faith, one baptism, one God and Father of us all, who is above all and through all and in all."

If the Church has failed to love sufficiently, it is because we as individuals have not loved enough. The Body of Christ is not an organization; it is a people, God's people. Only individuals are converted. Only individuals are holy. Only individuals love or hate. "Christianity is less attractive than it ought to be because my love is less believable than it ought to be. [I have to] stop thinking that it is the person next to me, or the previous generation, or the bishop or the institutional church that is lacking in love."[3]

In April '86, I had a shattering experience. An angry student at an evangelical college shouted at me: "How dare you claim to be a Christian and still be a Catholic?" I went home and asked myself: How often in the last ten years have I wept over the tragic disunity in the broken Body of Christ? Do you know, I could not remember one. It was then that I wept—not for the student—but for me.

The ecumenical ebb is a sad consequence of our lovelessness. The tide of initiative, which once promised to permeate every level of church life, is slowly washing out into a sea of indifference. Many of us feel threatened by the ecumenical principle of reciprocity, which implies a single enterprise among equal partners qualified by the individual commitment to faith. The ecumenical movement is neither a father-son nor a haves-and-have-nots relationship. It is dialogue on the grassroots level, and this involves risk: it means that all parties may be changed in the process and may not come out the same. In a conversation among equals, Romans, Baptists, evangelicals, Pentecostals, Episcopalians, Methodists, Lutherans, and so on allow themselves to be challenged and called into question. In prayer meetings and worship assemblies all parties are prepared to grow and to change in a gentle interplay of giving and receiving.

Though the ecumenical principle of authenticity presupposes a commitment to one's own faith tradition (the antithesis of collective bargaining or compromise), many of us still fear that interfaith dialogue will tend to lessen the distinctive elements of our particular heritage, and to soften vigorous and forthright assertions on the unique character of our faith community.

"We would like to renew our own church," Ralph Martin writes, "and not go through the personal and corporate changes necessary for union with other churches. We would still like to think of our Christian brothers and sisters in other churches as 'them' rather than 'us.' It hurts less; it requires less change. But God will stop with nothing less than the full restoration and reunion with his people, and those who want to stop short of that run the risk of being left behind in the desert to die."[4]

The *discipline of the secret* discourages massive ecumenical rallies at least for the next decade. On the grassroots level it calls for Christian interface with an attitude of openness and mutual respect, seeking what is decisive and distinctive about discipleship and discovering what is common to the separated Christian churches. If we are open-minded, we challenge fixed ideas and established structures, including our own. We listen to people in other denominations and fellowships and are receptive to other ways of thinking. We do not find demons in those with whom we disagree or conclude they must be living in sin. The humble disciple realizes that God's truth cannot be imprisoned in a small definition.

The future of Christian reunion is a work of love. As the Irish are fond of saying: "A soft word never yet broke a tooth." Real reform and renewal in the Body of Christ must include a reconciliation among all Christians. Furthermore, contemporary ecumenism must reach out with love and a servant's heart to the other great world religions—Judaism, Islam, Hinduism, and Buddhism. The goal is not some sterile philosophical concept of "universal religion" but a genuine reverence and respect for the pursuit of truth wherever we encounter it, and however far from the goal others appear to us to be.

Jesus says, "The kingdom of heaven is like a dragnet cast into the sea that brings in a haul of all kinds. When it is full, the fishermen haul it ashore; then, sitting down, they collect the good ones in a basket and throw away those that are no use. This is how it will be at the end of time: the angels will appear and separate the wicked from the just to throw them into the blazing furnace where there will be weeping and grinding of teeth" (Matthew 13:47–50, JB). If Jesus is willing to wait until the end of time to begin the sorting process, how dare we be so eager to categorize, separate, and reject before the time appointed? We need to pray for more of the divine forbearance in our lives.

While I was in ministry in California, a 23-year-old girl came to me in great distress. She was filled with fear that her father was not saved. "He goes to church every Sunday," she said, "but he's not into the Word, and as far as I know, he has not accepted Jesus Christ as Lord and Savior." When I asked her to describe her father's manner of life, she replied, "He's the most wonderful dad any girl could have. He and my mother have a wonderful marriage. He's so kind and thoughtful—but that's not the point. How can he be saved if he hasn't confessed Jesus as Lord?"

Aware that my reply to her question may not harmonize with certain Christian traditions, I shall present another viewpoint, inviting the reader to separate the wheat from the chaff of my own limited vision. In actual experience we rarely live in an either/or world: either creation or evolution, liberty or law, God or man, home or career, Beethoven or Bruce Springsteen. Like the Church in its highest tradition, we focus on both/and. The following reflections are borne of an urgent pastoral need in the Christian community. They address directly this young girl's inquiry as well as the salvation of non-Christians and unbelievers. My intent is not to create controversy but to raise consciousness as we explore the dimensions of the dragnet.

For those of us who claim the Name, it is critical to understand that the signature of Jesus Christ liberates us from narrow and confining versions of religion. For the cross is not about religion, but about the power of God.

Thomas Merton wrote: "The cross is a sign of contradiction—destroying the seriousness of the law, of the Empire, of the armies. . . . But the magicians keep turning the cross to their own purposes [with] the awful blasphemy of the religious magician who makes the cross contradict mercy! That is of course the ultimate temptation of Christianity. To say that Christ has locked all the doors, has given one answer, settled everything and departed, leaving all life closed in the frightful consistency of a system outside of which there is seriousness and damnation, inside of which there is the intolerable flippancy of the saved—while nowhere is there any place left for the mystery of the freedom of divine mercy. . . ."[5]

Erich Fromm wrote about "the escape from freedom" as a characteristic of our time. Merton has identified the particular escape from this threatening freedom, which has enticed too many Christian minds—the tendency to draw tight the boundaries of salvation, to create a system of beliefs and practices that denies the radical freedom of God's mercy to move where it will, within the Church and without.

In the parable of the wheat and the weeds (Matthew 13:24–30) Jesus tells us that human beings are not capable of carrying out the separation of good and bad. In the early stages of growth, the wheat and the weeds resemble each other. So too among the people of God, true disciples and fakers are mingled together. With our inherent limitations, we humans cannot discern the heart of another. If we attempt to separate the saved and the unsaved (or the washed and the unwashed, as some Pentecostals say), we will inevitably commit errors of judgment and root up good wheat with the weeds. Jesus says pointedly: "Judge not, and you will not be judged." And He means this for all time! It is the angels, not we human beings, even the elect, who will toss out the worthless fish at the end of the age, in the parable of the dragnet.

Paul writes: "There must be no passing of premature judgment. Leave that until the Lord comes: he will light up all that is hidden in the dark and reveal the secret intentions of men's hearts. Then will be the time for each one to have whatever praise he deserves from God" (1 Corinthians 4:5, JB).

During an interview shortly before his death in 1980, the influential German theologian Karl Rahner observed that it is traditional Catholic teaching that all who follow their consciences are accepted by God, even if they think themselves unbelievers, and "can reach that eternal life we confess in our Christian faith as the goal of all."

But what of the many New Testament passages (Mark 16:16, Acts 4:12; John 14:6, 1 Timothy 2) that seem to contradict this open-ended view of salvation and point to a narrower interpretation of God's saving activity in the world? They mention an explicit confession of Jesus Christ as Lord and Savior as the condition for salvation.

Yet, as Thomas Hart states in his splendid book *To Know and Follow Jesus*,[6] there are other New Testament texts that support a less exclusivist view of salvation:

"And opening his mouth, Peter said: 'I most certainly understand now that God is not one to show partiality, but in every nation the man that fears Him and does what is right, is welcome to Him" (Acts 10:34–35, NAS).

"For it is not those who hear the law who are righteous in God's sight, but it is those who obey the law who will be declared righteous. (Indeed, when Gentiles, who do not have the law, do by nature things required by the law, they are a law for themselves . . . since they show that the requirements of the law are written in their hearts, their consciences also bearing witness, and their thoughts now accusing, now even defending them.) This will take place on the day when God will judge men's secrets through Jesus Christ" (Romans 2:13–16, NIV).

"God is love, and the one who abides in love abides in God, and God abides in him" (1 John 4:16, NAS).

148

"These texts loosen the hold of the exclusivist position and of the fear or fanaticism that sometimes attends that position."[7] They speak directly to the 23-year-old California girl frightened over her father's salvation. They depict a God whose saving design is universal, and the signs of whose saving grace are perceivable outside the Christian community. In holding to this more open view of the dimensions of the dragnet and the sweep of God's mercy and grace, Christians of course maintain that where there is salvation, it is due to the death and resurrection of Jesus Christ even if He is not acknowledged. The quality of a person's life may point to the presence and activity of Christ's saving grace even when the source is not recognized.

Let us take the classic situation of a tribe of pygmies living in the trackless forests of Africa. They have never been visited by a Christian missionary and have never heard the name of Jesus Christ. Yet they live faithfully by their primitive tribal code, which honors a higher power as the Source of life: They worship the sun god four times a year. Further, the code imposes obligations toward parents, and forbids incest and stealing. The pygmies live by these moral precepts. The tenor of their lives is fidelity to the limited truth they have received. They live honestly according to their consciences. One can presume that if they were given the fullness of the revelation of God in Jesus Christ, they would accept it because the pattern of their lives is adherence to truth. Implicit Christianity is at work in the pygmies' lives. They are baptized by their desire for Truth who they do not know is Jesus. Thus, salvation comes to their house.

"Karl Rahner is well known for his theology of implicit or anonymous Christianity. It is derived from the two basic ideas in his Christology: the human person as the mystery of infinite emptiness and God as the mystery of infinite fulness. God is at the horizon in the life of every person, experienced at the edge of consciousness. God reaches out graciously to every person, and is at least dimly known by every person as that mysterious power in human life that both challenges and comforts. Whenever any person is open to that mystery and responds to it, in attitudes and choices, that person displays faith, even if he or she does not acknowledge God or Christ by name.

"Those who have [this implicit faith] are hopeful even in the midst of adversity. . . . They apply themselves to their daily responsibilities, take care of their families, transcend selfishness in their relationships with at least some people in their world. By these manifestations of hope and love, we know the presence of their . . . yes-saying to God."[8]

Rahner's definition of "anonymous Christian" for those persons who respond to the inner voice of God in their lives without an explicit Christian commitment implies that the divine dragnet has indeed been cast wide. It invites us to a radical trust in God until the Final Judgment, which definitively ushers in the Kingdom of God.

This theological position avoids the trap of *universalism*, which holds that all persons will be saved regardless of their personal response to God's unconditional love. Universalism is a non-Christian cast of thought that makes moral choices unnecessary and the death-resurrection of Jesus Christ irrelevant to man's restoration to God.

The commission entrusted to the Church is to proclaim that God's love knows no bounds, that there is a God who loves us beyond imagining. The Kingdom of God is larger than the Church. The two are not co-extensive. No Christian can ever make any legitimate presumption about the spiritual state of another man or woman. The Spirit of God blows where He will; the Christian Church claims no monopoly on grace, holds no franchise for salvation. The God of Christianity is a tad bigger than that.

The prophet Jonah is a classic example of religious exclusivity. His myopia encased God in a narrow nationalism. God was *his* God, the God of the Hebrews, enshrined in one Temple, one Ark of the Covenant. Jonah was not a bad guy. He was a religious man who was willing to drown for pagan sailors. Yet he could let thousands of human beings perish in their unbelief without a blush.

The prophetic message of the book of Jonah is a warning to all of us. The author was saying in effect: "Each of you is Jonah—dreadfully nearsighted. Remember your vocation, the universal vocation of Israel: to preach to the nations the endless breadth of God's mercy and forgiveness. Recall the calling of Abraham, representative of Israel: 'By you all the families of the earth shall be blessed' (Genesis 12:3). Recollect God's word through Isaiah: 'I have given you as a covenant to the people, a light to the nations, to open the eyes that are blind' (Isaiah 42:6–7), 'that my salvation may reach to the ends of the earth' (Isaiah 49:6). The meaning of Jonah? God's loving mercy waits for all who repent, whoever they are, wherever they live, whatever they have done."[9]

Today some people believe that only Christians will graze heaven's green pastures. Such is not our God. Our God, the New Testament insists, "longs for all to be saved" (1 Timothy 2:4, LB). This past year the world celebrated the birth of its five billionth inhabitant. Of that mighty human army, approximately one-third is Christian. If we hold to the exclusivist position that there is no salvation except through an explicit faith-commitment to Jesus Christ, then more than three billion people currently alive are damned! We are face-to-face with a distinctly unpleasant deity. What kind of God is this "who creates the vast majority of human beings for eternal damnation?"[10] Do not we Christians proclaim a God of relentless tenderness as well as holiness?

The making of this proclamation, the Christian missionary enterprise, remains not only intact but doubly urgent to those who have glimpsed the all-inclusive scope of

God's intent. The responsibility of bearing Christian witness is Gospel imperative. Jesus says: "You will be my witnesses. I have chosen you from the world to go and bear fruit." Only at the price of losing its identity and ceasing to be, could the Christian community withdraw from its mission to serve the entire human family and to bear witness, by word and deed, to the healing power of Jesus before all peoples, everywhere, to the end of time. Failure in that witness is failure to be Jesus' disciple. "But in fidelity to that same Christ and Christ's pedagogy, Christians in their witness should shun all conversionary attitudes and practices that do not conform to the way a free God freely draws individuals to serve in spirit and truth."[11]

If salvation is open to those who live according to their consciences with all rectitude, certain approaches to the Christian mission must be reexamined. All non-Christians are not depraved sinners in bondage to Satan. When we see the values of the Gospel reflected in their lives, they are to be congratulated by the missionary: "You are doing what we speak of." When a non-Christian is seen to be living for his brothers and sisters, pouring himself out in a life of service, the Gospel is meant to encounter him not with condemnation but with commendation. He is living in grace. "Too much woe has come from our coming at non-Christians with eyes shut and mouth open, bent on gifting grace to a graceless world.

"There is a further misfortune. By fancying itself as God's unique channel of salvation, the Church inevitably degenerates into institutional egotism. Leaders tend to fret about Church growth and attendance at services, losing sight of the more substantial signs of the growth or decline of human compassion, wisdom and love, which are really the telltale indices of grace in the world. The Church's main task is not to spread the Church; it is to spread faith and love and service. People who heed the message will coagulate and group into the Church, but this is not the purpose; it is a byproduct. The Church is not sent into the world with an uncommon work to do. It is sent with an uncommon insight from revelation to join in a most common work: salvation."[12]

The missionary is a leaven in the mass. Excited about Jesus, she encourages sinners to repent and invites the righteous to discover how they came to be so and how much more they might be. Nevertheless, she is not preoccupied with the head count. Many of the effects of her efforts may not be immediately detected. As always, "the grain of wheat must fall into the ground and die. If it dies, it bears much fruit." It is not uncommon that contact with a devout Muslim or Buddhist can lead the missionary to be a better Christian.

Charles deFoucauld, who founded the Little Brothers of Jesus (the community I lived with in Europe for two years), reported that his dormant Christian faith sprang to life when he joined the French Foreign Legion. One day, his platoon was engaged in a heavy rifle exchange with an enemy battalion of Muslims. Because of the overwhelming number of Muslims and their superior weapons, death was imminent for the platoon of Legionnaires. But as the sun went down, the Muslims laid down their rifles to worship Allah and deFoucauld and his comrades slipped away in the darkness. He was so shaken by the Muslims' faith and reckless disregard for the outcome of the combat, that he embarked on his own spiritual journey that led to complete surrender to Jesus Christ.

According to recent polls, the number of those who call themselves atheists is diminishing. Attendance at Madalyn Murray O'Hair's national convention dropped conspicuously this past year. Of the handful of atheists I have met in my travels, none rejected the idea of a Supreme Being per se. Rather their incredulity could be traced to the shabby lifestyle of some Christian they knew.

Early in Christian history St. Augustine complained, "Many who had already come close on the way to believing are frightened away by the bad lives of evil and false Christians. How many, my brothers, do you think there are who want to become Christians but are put off by the evil ways of Christians?" If the seeker after truth finds Christian people to be just as self-absorbed, guilt-ridden, fearful, and unsure of their foundations as he is, small wonder he feels no attraction for the Christian message.

A student doing graduate work at the University of Paris wrote: "To me a Christian is a person who either lives in Christ or is a phony. You Christians do not appreciate that it is on this—the almost external testimony that you give of God—that we judge you. You ought to radiate Christ. Your faith ought to flow out to us like a river of life. You ought to infect us with a love for him. It is then that the God who was impossible becomes possible for the atheist and for those of us whose faith is wavering. We cannot help being struck, upset and confused by a Christian who is truly Christlike. And we do not forgive when you fail to be."

The student is reiterating what Emmanuel Suhard wrote in a pastoral letter in 1947: "The great mark of a Christian is what no other characteristic can replace—namely, the example of a life which can only be explained in terms of God." We will never win unbelievers to Jesus Christ merely by making speeches about Him. Contact with Christians should be an experience that proves to men and women that the Gospel has life-transforming power.

One Japanese atheist utterly rejected a God who has a special affection for Americans. He was told by an evangelical patriot from North Carolina that the bomb dropped on Hiroshima vaporizing 95,000 women, children, and older men was the will of God because it saved the lives of American "boys."

How often in the past our dialogue with atheists and

members of other religions has been calculated to drive away rather than to win? As Hart describes it: "We believe we are in contact with God, and we are right; you believe you are in contact with God but you are wrong."[13]

Is this the mind of Christ? Did the Master not say, "By their fruits you shall know them," not by their theological positions and creedal statements?

In a world of religious diversity, the Spirit of Jesus calls us to an attitude of reverence, meaning that we acknowledge the right of the other to exist and be what he or she is. Jesus saw good in the unlikeliest places and offered people what they need most—encouragement for their lives.

God's truth cannot be imprisoned in our grasp of it or caged by our tiny minds. The apparent contradictions of the New Testament are transformed into paradox if we can learn to love the questions even when we don't have the answers. "The poles of either/or, the choices we thought we had to make between saved and unsaved, may become signs of a larger truth than we had ever dreamed. And in that truth, our lives may become larger than we had ever imagined possible."[14]

We must learn to love the questions—and to repudiate the non-questions. The familiar objection, "Then what's unique about Christianity?" is simply a non-issue for those of us on the Way. Let me put this as bluntly as possible: Only the person who has never experienced the overwhelming love of Jesus Christ would bother to ask, "If others can be saved, what's the point of being a Christian?" Only the person who has never tasted the peace that the world cannot find would ask, "Why be a Christian?" Only the person who does not realize that what is at stake in the transaction is eternity would say, "I guess one religion is as good as another."

Contemporary ecumenism embraces both our separated Christian brothers and sisters and seekers after truth of every background. It is never based on irresponsible relativism.

The dimensions of the dragnet is a burning theological issue in the divided Body of Christ. Some Christian denominations tend to pull the drawstrings tight and deny the freedom of the Spirit to blow where He will. Personally, I believe that all salvation comes through Jesus Christ and that His saving grace is at work even when He is not explicitly acknowledged. My faith experience of Abba-God and His Christ leads me to believe in the salvation of non-Christians who live according to their consciences with full rectitude. No limitations must ever be placed on the cosmic Lordship of Jesus. While I firmly believe in heaven and hell, I cannot accept that the greater part of the human adventure will fail; that the Father's only plan—Jesus Christ—will be defeated in the lives of the vast majority of men and women. My faith is not a well-rehearsed set of Scriptural quotations. It is a radical trust that God will finish what He started, that His wisdom and mercy are so far beyond anything I can intellectualize or imagine, that on the Last Day I will only blink, gasp, and weep for joy.

Nine

The Courage
to Risk

The story of the first Pentecost is a familiar one. Fifty days after Easter, the disciples were gathered together in one place. Suddenly they were engulfed in a mighty wind and startled by flames of fire resting on each of them. They were filled with the Spirit and power to speak to Passover pilgrims from many lands and be understood in their local languages. Though dramatic, this story is easy to follow and also to visualize.

Whenever the Spirit of God breaks into our lives, in the middle of the day, in the middle of the week, or the middle of a lifetime, it is to announce in some fashion that the time for pussyfooting is over. The mighty rushing wind of the first Pentecost symbolized that something new and wonderful was coming to pass by the power of God. Just as a band of timid, inactive, evasive, and helpless disciples were transformed into fearless, articulate witnesses, so with us. When we are seized by the power of a great affection, we are empowered with the courage to risk. The Spirit sets us free from our self-imposed limits and moves us out into uncharted waters. Our secure, well-regulated, and largely risk-free lives are blown apart. The Spirit saves us from "both our high idealism (with all its ego investment) and our low self-esteem (with its even more intense ego investment) and lifts us beyond our utmost bounds to undreamed of possibilities, to the idealism of God Himself."[1]

The response of Peter and the others was uninspiring, flawed by fear and hesitation. The track record of the Twelve was poor: They complained, they quarreled, they wavered, they deserted. The biography of these apostolic stalwarts was one of wary, inconsistent discipleship. Yet, God's free use of flawed people to accomplish His purpose is a resounding affirmation to those of us trapped in feelings of inadequacy and inferiority. As Alan Jones has noted, "The most difficult thing in mature believing is to accept that I am an object of God's delight."

More often than I like to admit, I still get bamboozled into trying to make myself acceptable to God. It seems I cannot forgo this crazy enterprise of getting myself into a position where I can see myself in a good light. I still struggle to let go of the preposterous pretense that my paltry prayers, knowledge of Scripture, spiritual insights, tithing to the poor, and blustering successes in ministry endear me to God's eyes. I find robust inner resistance to the saving truth that I am lovable simply and solely because He loves me.

Anyone caught up in the same oppression of self-justification understands what I am saying. In our own way we are as absurd as the character in the Agatha Christie novel who cannot imagine heaven as being anything else but an occasion to make herself useful—little imagining that everybody else in heaven is struggling to endure the unceasing persecution of her devoted service. Will we ever be free of the Pelagian fantasy that we save ourselves? Will we ever accept little Elam Zook as a replica of the love of Jesus Christ?

In pensive moments, I wonder if I really have the courage to risk everything on the Gospel of grace and accept the total sufficiency of Christ's redeeming work. My futile attempts at self-improvement, the sadness that I am not yet perfect, the subtle boasting about my victories in the vineyard, my sensitivity to criticism and lack of self-acceptance belie my profession of faith, "Jesus is Lord." Lip service from a shackled servant still in bondage to the insecurity that wears a thousand masks, still lacking the courage to risk all on Him who is all, still thrashing about trying to fix myself, still struggling for that elusive achievement that will make me presentable to God. Brennan the basket case! False modesty? No, otherwise, why was I rattled when after a sermon I preached in Chapel Hill, North Carolina, evangelist Tommy Tyson looked up with tears in his eyes and said: "Something wonderful just happened to me: I know as I have never known before that what Jesus did was enough."

On that overcast afternoon I decided to put my do-it-yourself kit in a garage sale, jettison some heavy cargo I had been carrying, and hearken to the words of Robert M. Brown: "Be it hereby enacted: That every three years all people shall forget whatever they have learned about Jesus, and begin the study all over again."[2]

The Spirit convicted Peter that he was not doomed to repeat the mistakes of the past. Nor are we. There is a power available to transcend our automatic emotional responses and robot-like behavior. Endowed with the courage to risk everything on the truth of the Gospel, we surrender our gnawing need to be okay and cease applying spiritual cosmetics to make ourselves presentable.

And yet . . . the prospect frightens us. We'd like to stay close enough to the fire to keep warm but are reluctant to dive in. We know we will come out burnt, incandescently transformed. Life will never be the same again. Nonetheless, we are dissatisfied with the narrow dimensions of our partial commitment. Deep within there is a longing to throw caution to the winds. We know that what Leon Bloy said is true: "The only real sadness in life is not to be a saint."

Graham Greene wrote a telling novel entitled *The Power and the Glory*. The central character is the "whiskey priest," a sad man, lax, tepid, and alcoholic. At the moment he is about to be executed by a firing squad, he realizes it would have been easy to be a saint if he had had the courage to risk. For years the inner robot had controlled his outer life. Looking into the barrels of five loaded rifles, he perceived that his weakness was only hypochondria. A few hours earlier, he had walked across this courtyard and nothing he saw seemed to matter. Long ago he had bartered courage and freedom for passivity and trivialities. Were his execution delayed and he could walk back across the courtyard, he would be wide-eyed with wonder. Puddles would seem like oceans, soldiers like gods. With his inner robot suppressed and his automatic emotions no longer in command, he would lay hold of his life, grasp it 'round the neck, and move in the conviction that to live without risk is to risk not living.

In the power of a great affection the impossible becomes possible. We are freed from the fears that lock us in the paralysis of analysis. We know we can't lose because we have nothing to lose.

Nothing is more puzzling to me than our massive resistance to the inbreak of God's love. Why are we so churlish to receive? Are we afraid of becoming vulnerable, of losing control of our lives, of acknowledging our weakness and need? Do we keep God at a safe distance to protect the illusion of our independence?

The parable of the unforgiving debtor (Matthew 18) offers a clue. He owes his master the sum of ten thousand talents—the equivalent of the national debt. What does he do? Does he cast himself on the mercy of his merciful master, admit his total helplessness in the situation, and beg forgiveness? Absolutely not. The debtor is not into admitting inadequacy. He is a man of substance and consequence. He has credentials and credit cards. Honors have been conferred upon him. His ego has been stroked. His dignity is intact.

In the most preposterous statement in all four Gospels, he says to his master: "Look here, you are a reasonable man. You know the stock market is mercurial. I just ran into a streak of bad luck. Give me a little time and I will repay the national debt." Being realistic, his master instead forgives the entire amount. But the debtor, of course, misses the freeing import of this incredible generosity. He hadn't asked for any favors! He'd been going to repay that impossible sum through his own efforts. And because he could not receive forgiveness, he could not extend it to his fellow servant who owed him a paltry sum.[3]

This false sense of self, brimming with pride and pretense, must die if we are to live. The constant challenge in this life we call Christian is the translation of what we believe into our day-to-day lifestyle. Risky business! When that little icon of Jesus buried his lips into mine in unself-conscious freedom, I was empowered to do something I had never done before in my life: kiss another man on the lips and to hell with propriety. The love of Jesus Christ frees us from all stiffness and protocol.

This doesn't, of course, mean conforming to some prescribed pattern of enthusiastic affection, such as a variety of modern movements are eager to impose. Rather, it is a thing of complete spontaneity, unprogrammed and unpredictable. It is more likely to make us feel foolish (if we are the least bit self-conscious) than to make us feel that at last we have arrived at Christian maturity. In order to do more than adopt a passing fad, we never forget that the spontaneous affection erupting within us is the love of God poured into our hearts by the Holy Spirit. The courage to risk approaching an enemy to seek reconciliation belongs in the same category. It will expose us to very probable rejection, ridicule, and failure.

In retrospect, the landmark moments in my life are not the gross sins I committed nor the infrequent acts of heroic virtue I performed, but a handful of decisions that involved risk: the decision to seek ordination to the priesthood, to join the Little Brothers of Jesus, to live in a cave, to seek help for my addiction to alcohol, to marry. On the last day when we stand before the risen Christ, *each of us will be the sum of our choices.*

Mister Blue was a daring gentleman who lived at ease with music and balloons on an apartment house roof. He moved gracefully with all kinds of people in poverty and abundance and refused to be tied down to the standards of others. In the evening of his life, Mister Blue wrote: "Conservative historians describe any man with a passion for greatness as a megalomaniac. 'Look at him,' they say to one another, 'the idiot! Why doesn't he settle down and establish himself in the community? Why is he forever restless, forever trying to get something beyond him? The man is crazy.'

"These conservatives are partly right. Play life safe and you will keep out of harm. Be careful, be cautious, don't take risks and you will never die on Mount St. Helens. Your failure is measured by your aspirations. Aspire not, and you cannot fail. Columbus died in chains. Joan of Arc was burned at the stake. Let us all live snugly without risk, and life will soon be little more than a thick gelatinous stream of comfortability and ignorance."[4]

The restlessness of the fictional Mister Blue echoes the parable of Jesus on the unprofitable servant (Luke 17:7–10). It recalls the deathbed exhortation of Francis of

Assisi, "Let us begin, my brothers, for up to now we have done but little." Blue can be heard in the gentle voice of my friend Tom Minifie, an associate pastor in Seattle: "To be at ease is to be unsafe." The *ekklesia* of the Lord Jesus starts to decay when the members who comprise it forfeit their willingness to risk.

Every college president recognizes that some academic departments are enjoying exceptional vitality while others merely drone along. Every businessman observes that some firms are on their toes while others are in a rut. The same factors are at work in the rise and fall of any enterprise, including the Church's. Rome falling to the barbarians, an old family firm going into bankruptcy, a government agency strangling in its own red tape, a church dying of spiritual consumption all have a great deal in common.

When an institution is young, it is flexible, fluid, not yet paralyzed by rigid specialization, willing to try anything once. As the institution ages, risk-taking decreases, daring gives way to rigidity, creativity fades, the capacity to meet new challenges from unexpected directions is lost.

The same processes at work in the demise of institutions likewise operate in the decline of individuals. "Why is it," John Gardner asks, "that so many people are mummified by the time of middle age?" Why do some people settle into rigid and unchanging views on God and Church by the time they are thirty years old? Why do we fall into a stupor of mind and spirit long before we are golden girls and boys? Is it inevitable that we surrender our youthfulness and our capacity to grow and change? Is personal renewal, the seedbed of community renewal, possible?

I read somewhere that the late General Douglas MacArthur once wrote: "Youth is not a period of time. It is a state of mind, a result of the will, a quality of the imagination, a victory of courage over timidity, of the taste for adventure over the love of comfort. A man does not grow old simply because he has lived a certain number of years. A man becomes old when he has deserted his ideal. The years wrinkle his skin, but deserting his ideal wrinkles his soul. Preoccupations, fears, doubts and despair are the enemies which slowly bow us toward earth, and turn us into dust before death. You will remain young as long as you are receptive to what is beautiful, good, great; receptive to the messages of men and women, of nature and of God. If one day you should become bitter and pessimistic and gnawed by despair, may God have mercy on your old man's soul."

Perhaps the major cause of failure in individual and community renewal is the very fear of failure itself. We avoid risk so as not to be shown up as mistaken before the world. The tyranny of our peers (what will others say?) immobilizes us. Wise and prudent people that we are, we manufacture a thousand logical excuses for doing nothing.

The fear of falling on our faces exacts a heavy price. It discourages exploration and assures the progressive narrowing of the personality. There is no learning without fumbling. If we are to keep growing, we must risk failure all our lives. When Max Planck was awarded the Nobel Prize for the formulation of the Quantum theory, he said: "Looking back over the long and labyrinthine path which finally led to the discovery, I am vividly reminded of Goethe's saying that men will always be making mistakes as long as they are striving after something."

Although Christianity is all about redemption from sin and failure, the majority of us (based on my pastoral experience) are unwilling to admit to failure in our lives. Partially this is due to human nature's defense mechanisms against its own inadequacies. Even more, it can be traced to the success image our current Christian culture demands of us. Once converted we no longer dare lose our businesses, our marriages, or our figures.

The problem with projecting the perfect image, however, is that it creates more problems than it solves. First, it is simply not true: None of us is always joyful, unruffled, and in command. Second, projecting the flawless image distances us from other people who conclude we would not understand them. Third, even if we could live a life free of risk and mistakes, it would be a shallow existence. Mature Christians are those who have failed and learned to live gracefully with their failure.

Our failure to have done with our lives what we longed to accomplish weighs heavy on most of us. The disparity between our ideal self and our real self, the specter of past infidelities, the awareness that my behavior often flatly denies my beliefs, the relentless pressure of conformity, and our nostalgia for lost innocence reinforces a nagging sense of existential guilt: I have failed. This is the cross we never expected, the one we find hardest to bear. We can no longer differentiate between our perception of ourselves and the mystery we really are.[5]

The pernicious myth "once converted, fully converted" creates the impression that in one blinding bolt of salvation Christ expects our lives to be freed from contradictions and perplexities. The curse of perfectionism triggers episodes of depression and anxiety. Who will acquit us of guilt? Who will deliver us from the bondage of perfectionism and failure? Once again, it is the signature of Jesus that rescues us from ourselves.

The crucified Christ reminds us that despair and disillusionment are not terminal but signs of impending resurrection. What lives beyond the cross is the liberating power of love, freeing us from the ego-centeredness that says, "All I am is what I think I am and nothing more." One Good Friday morning at two A.M., as I prayed before a symbol of the Crucified, in faith I heard Him say, "Little brother, I witnessed a Peter who claimed that he did not know Me, a James who wanted power in return for service, a Philip who failed to see the Father in Me, and scores of disciples who were convinced I was finished on Calvary. The New Testament has many examples of men and women who started out well and then faltered along the way.

"Yet on Easter night I appeared to Peter; James is not remembered for his ambition but for the sacrifice of his life for the Kingdom; Philip did see the Father in Me when I pointed the way, and the disciples who despaired had enough courage to recognize Me as the stranger who walked the road to Emmaus. My point, little brother, is this: I expect more failure from you than you expect from yourself."

In season and out of season, in success and failure, in grace and disgrace, the courage to risk everything on the signature of Jesus is the mark of authentic discipleship. In the words of Winston Churchill: "Success is never final; failure is never fatal. It is courage that counts."

Ten

The Time
to Pray

Newsweek magazine, in a feature essay of its March 12, 1979, issue commemorating the centennial of Albert Einstein's birth, assembled the following account:

"In the beginning . . . a fireball of pure energy exploded, cooling as it spread outward; in one-hundredth of a second after creation, the temperature of the universe was one hundred billion degrees Celsius and its density almost four billion times that of water. Particles emerged [and] held together long enough to create hydrogen and helium nuclei. A half-hour later, one quarter of the hydrogen had changed into helium, determining forever the chemical constitution of the universe.

". . . The nuclei and electrons combined to form stable hydrogen and helium gas. Soon the clouds of gas coalesced into stars and galaxies."[1]

This scientific account staggers the mind. The patience of God in fashioning one planet capable of human habitation is almost incomprehensible. In reply to the question "Why would God go to such incredible lengths to create a home for His people?", faith answers, "Because He loves us." The simplicity of the answer is the key to interpreting sacred Scripture, for the Bible is the love story of God with mankind.

Should you ask, "Why do I exist? What am I doing walking around this planet earth?", you must answer, "Because I have been loved by God." If the angels ask why they exist, they must cry out, "Because we have been loved by God." If the whole universe were suddenly to become articulate, the stones would shout, "We exist because we have been loved by God." That cry would issue from the seas and the rivers. It would be tapped out by the pattering rain. It would be written in the skies by lightning. The storms would roar the love of God and the mountains would echo it back. The sun on its westward march through the heavens would chant a thunderous hymn, "I exist because I have been loved by God." To press for some ponderous philosophical explanation for the mystery of human existence is to deprive God of the simplest explanation of all, namely that He is love.

William Reiser writes: "Many parents have waited years for their children to acknowledge that they have been loved. There are many times, naturally, when mothers and fathers find their patience exhausted by children who seem to take them for granted and rarely give a thought to their parents' feelings. Yet somehow, parents retain faith in their children, because they believe that so much care and love spent on them must one day bear fruit. Parents live in hope for the day when a child will realize what love it has received. I remember a father confiding to me that he would give anything he had in order to have his son come home one day and throw his arms, not around his father (that would have been too much to hope for) but around his mother, and tell her, 'I love you.' "[2]

When children acknowledge the love that has been lavished on them, it puts a bloom on the day. The experience of being appreciated resonates deep within us and numbers among the happiest moments we ever enjoy. Is it farfetched to imagine God experiencing the same thing? He longs for children who gratefully acknowledge how deeply they have been loved.

One day Rabbi Barukh's grandson Yehiel was playing hide-and-seek with another boy. He hid himself well and waited for his playmate to find him. After twenty minutes, he peeked out of his secret hiding place, saw no one, and pulled his head back inside. After waiting a very long time, he came out of his hiding place but the other boy was nowhere to be seen. Then Yehiel realized that his playmate had not looked for him from the very beginning. Crying, he ran to his grandfather and complained of his faithless friend. Tears brimmed in Rabbi Barukh's eyes as he realized: God says the same thing: I hide but no one wants to seek Me.[3]

Such was the poignant tone when God spoke through His prophet Hosea: "When Israel was a child, I loved him, and out of Egypt I called my son. But the more I called Israel, the further they went from me. They sacrificed to the Baals and they burned incense to images. It was I who taught Ephraim to walk, taking them by the arms; but they did not realize it was I who healed them. I led them with cords of human kindness, with ties of love. I lifted the yoke from their neck and bent down to feed them" (Hos. 11:1–4, NIV).

Our God remains a hidden God; but in prayer we discover that we have what we seek. We start from where we are, discover what we have and realize we are already there. We are not searching for something we do not have. Prayer is simply experiencing what we already possess.

"Are you not aware," Paul writes, "that you are the temple of God, and that the Spirit of God dwells in you?" The wondrous thing is that God wants to be found more than we want to seek Him. "When you seek me you shall find me, when you seek me with all your heart; I will let you find me (—it is Yahweh who speaks)" (Jeremiah 29:13–14, JB).

Whatever else it may be, prayer is first and foremost a response to love. Beyond any pragmatic considerations, prayer is acknowledgment that we have been loved by God. To love someone implies a natural longing for presence and communion. Jesus prayed primarily because He loved His Father. Praise, adoration, thanksgiving, and intercession emanated from His profound awareness that His Abba is a God of love.

No matter how busy we are, we make time for those who are important to us. Simply *showing up* is a kind of loving. Basil Pennington captures this simplicity: "A father is delighted when his little one, leaving off his toys and friends, runs to him and climbs into his arms. As he holds his little one close to him, he cares little whether the child is looking around, his attention flitting from one thing to another, or just settling down to sleep. Essentially the child is choosing to be with his father, confident of the love, the care, the security, that is his in those arms. Our centering prayer is much like that. We settle down in our Father's arms, in his loving hands. Our mind, our thoughts, our imagination may flit about here and there; we might even fall asleep; but essentially we are choosing to remain for this time intimately with our Father, giving ourselves to him, receiving his love and care, letting him enjoy us as he will. It is very simple prayer. It is very childlike prayer. It is prayer that opens us out to all the delights of the Kingdom."[4]

"And when you pray, do not imitate the hypocrites: they love to say their prayers standing up in the synagogues and at the street corners for people to see them. I tell you solemnly, they have had their reward. But when you pray, go to your private room and, when you have shut your door, pray to your Father who is in that secret place, and your Father who sees all that is done in secret will reward you" (Matthew 6:5–6, JB). A disciplined life of daily prayer is an integral element of the *discipline of the secret*. It is our primary way to fulfill the great commandment to love God with all our heart, soul, mind, and strength. It is not a time-filler for the unemployed and elderly or a hobby for the idle. Jesus prayed when the demands on His time were heaviest. Luke tells us: "The news about Him was spreading . . . and great multitudes were gathering to hear Him and to be healed of their sicknesses. But He Himself would often slip away to the wilderness and pray" (Luke 5:15–16, NAS). Discipleship consists in looking at Jesus and doing what He did.

The most effective discipline I have found for making conscious contact with God is: forty minutes of prime time daily in solitary prayer, divided into two twenty-minute periods, morning and evening, before a symbol of the crucified Christ. The cross is the ultimate expression of God's love. A simple glance raises consciousness of how deeply we are loved and sets the tone of our prayer. Sit down. Sit still and upright. Close your eyes lightly. Be relaxed but alert. Silently, interiorly begin to say a single word. The Christian prayer word *Maranatha* whose Aramaic meaning is "Come, Lord Jesus" is a good one. Recite it in four syllables of equal length. Listen to it as you say it, gently but continuously. Never cease praying the word from beginning to end of the session. Do not think or imagine anything—spiritual or otherwise. If thoughts and images come, dismiss them without annoyance and return to simply saying the word. Intercessory and petitionary prayer can be done at another time during the day. Pray this way each morning and evening for a minimum of twenty minutes and a maximum of thirty.[5]

The tragedy in the Church today is that we have glibly

171

confused beliefs and faith, doctrines and lived experience. Daily prayer bridges the gap between belief and experience because it is the bridge of faith.

The cardinal rule in prayer is: One learns to pray by praying. What is vital is *showing up*, not simply thinking, talking, or reading about prayer. As Dom Bede Griffiths advises: "Pray as you can; don't pray as you can't." The method I have proposed is not the only way to pray; it has simply been tested in practice by many and is not unrelated to my personal experience. If it does not work, scrap it.

Don't pray just when you feel like it. This daily encounter with God should not be conditioned by our emotions. When we pray, our eyes are taken off ourselves. We discover that everything that happens to us is designed to teach us holiness. Most important is intensity of desire. When a disciple is hungry for God, he moves and acts, he is alive and responsive. He prays. He is not a diletante dabbling in spiritual things. To quote Rabbi Abraham Heschel: "God is of no importance unless He is of supreme importance."

The disciplined life of prayer is a courageous witness to the reality of the invisible God.

Eleven

Lazarus
Laughed!

One summer in Iowa City, Iowa, I directed a five-day retreat for a little band of Christians. The small number of retreatants allowed for an unusual degree of dialogue, sharing, and interpersonal communion. One mid-thirtyish woman in the group was conspicuous by her silence. She was a slender, attractive nun who neither smiled nor sighed, laughed nor cried, reacted, responded, nor communicated with any of us.

On the afternoon of the fourth day I invited each person to share what the Lord had been doing in his life the past few days. After a couple of minutes of silence, the uncommunicative nun (whom I shall call Christine) reached for her journal and said, "Something happened to me yesterday, and I wrote it down. You were speaking, Brennan, on the compassion of Jesus. You developed the

173

two images of husband and lover found in Isaiah 54 and Hosea 2. Then you quoted the words of St. Augustine, 'Christ is the best husband.'

"At the end of your talk, you prayed that we might experience what you had just shared. You asked us to close our eyes. Almost the moment I did, something happened. In faith I was transported into a large ballroom filled with people. I was sitting by myself on a wooden chair, when a man approached me, took my hand, and led me onto the floor. He held me in his arms and led me in the dance.

"The tempo of the music increased and we whirled faster and faster. The man's eyes never left my face. His radiant smile covered me with warmth, delight, and a sense of acceptance. Everyone else on the floor stopped dancing. They were staring at us. The beat of the music increased and we pirouetted around the room in reckless rhythm. I glanced at his hands, and then I knew. Brilliant wounds of a battle long ago, almost like a signature carved in flesh. The music tapered to a slow, lilting melody and Jesus rocked me back and forth. As the dance ended, he pulled me close to him. Do you know what he whispered?"

At this moment every retreatant in the chapel strained forward. Tears rolled down Christine's cheeks. A full minute of silence ensued. Though her face was beaming, the tears kept falling. Finally she spoke, "Jesus whispered to me, 'Christine, I'm wild about you.' "

She continued, "I stayed here in chapel for over an hour, then went to my room and began to write in my journal what I had just experienced. Suddenly it seemed as if the pen were lifted from my fingers. Again in faith I heard Jesus say, 'I'm really wild about you.' It was a *now* experience once more. The love of Jesus swept over me like a gentle tide saturating my being in wonder, bewilderment, peace, joy, certitude, and deep worship."

For Christine it was the release of the Holy Spirit

elevating her faith and love to a new plateau. It was a decisive breakthrough into a personal relationship with Christ as her husband and lover. Ignatius of Loyola would describe it as a moment of "immense consolation." Spiritual writers today would speak of a "mountaintop" experience, an encounter with "mysterium tremendum." Karl Rahner would simply call her a mystic—one who has experienced something.

What caught my attention in Christine's narrative was that the Jesus she encountered was smiling. Did Jesus smile? Did He actually laugh?

The Gospels never mention His doing either. They do testify that He wept twice—over Jerusalem and Lazarus, His city and His friend. Is it likely, however, that this sacred man, like us in all things but ungratefulness, could have wept from sorrow but not laughed for joy? Could Jesus have failed to smile when a child cuddled up in His arms, or when the headwaiter at Cana nearly fainted at the 600 gallons of vintage wine, or when He saw Zacchaeus out on a limb, or when Peter put his foot in his mouth one more time?

I simply cannot believe that Jesus did not laugh when He saw something funny or smile when He experienced in His being the love of His Abba. He attracted not only a leading Pharisee and a Roman centurion but children and simple folk like Mary Magdalene. Our human experience tells us that Jesus could not have done that if He always wore the solemn face of a mourner or the stern mask of a judge, if His face did not often crease into a smile and His whole body erupt in merry laughter.

Yet, how many paintings are there in the history of Christian art that portray a smiling Savior? Where in our songbooks and prayerbooks are there odes to a laughing Christ? We readily recall Him as "a man of sorrow" and forget how much joy His presence brought to sinners and partygoers, to the sick and the dying. Undoubtedly, Jesus laughed. He probably laughs at us when we rob disciple-ship of its playfulness and pull long faces like dignitaries at a state funeral.

Several years ago on a private retreat, I jotted down a short Easter meditation based on John 20:1–10. It reads: "Early Sunday morning, as the sun begins to streak across the eastern sky, the stiff body—the chest begins to heave—a hand moves up slowly and uncovers His face—He adjusts to the darkness—stands up shakily—passes out of the tomb. Outside, He breathes the fresh air—He thrills to His new experience—He looks up to the hill and sees three empty crosses. *He smiles and walks away.* The risen Christ is the smiling Christ."

Teresa of Avila wrote: "When the Lord showed himself to me, his body was always risen and glorified." Is it surprising that the Lord of glory who whirled Christine around the dance floor is a radiantly happy and smiling Christ?

Nevertheless, an intense Christian might protest: "Why is it important to establish whether Jesus smiled or not? It seems to me this is much ado about nothing. Let us move on to more urgent evangelical concerns."

The question of Jesus' joyfulness is not trivial for this reason: *Prayer is personal response to loving presence.* When the Jesus of our journey is the smiling Christ, when we respond to His whispered word, "I'm wild about you," the process of inner healing can begin. He heals us of our absorption in ourselves—where we take ourselves too seriously, where the days and nights revolve around us, our heartaches and hiatal hernias, our problems and frustrations. His smile allows us to distance ourselves from ourselves and see ourselves in perspective as we really are. We are creatures fearfully and wonderfully made, a bundle of paradoxes and contradictions. "We believe and doubt, hope and despair, love and hate. We are exciting and boring, enchanted and disillusioned, manic and depressive. We feel bad about feeling good; we are afraid of joy and feel guilty if we don't feel guilty. We are trusting and suspicious, selfless and selfish, wide-open and locked in. We know so much and so little. We are honest and still play games. Aristotle said we are rational animals. I say we are angels with an incredible capacity for beer."[1]

The story of the raising of Lazarus (John 11) begins with his two sisters, Martha and Mary, sending word to Jesus, "Lord, the man you love is ill."

When Jesus arrives in Bethany, Mary is told, "The Master is here and wants to see you." She goes to Jesus and throws herself at His feet saying, "Lord, if You had been here, my brother would not have died." At the sight of her tears, with a sigh that comes straight from His heart, Jesus asks: "Where is he?" She says, "Lord, come and see." Jesus weeps. And the Jews say, "See how much He loved him."

In 1981, Roslyn and I made a silent eight-day directed retreat at the renewal center in Grand Coteau, Louisiana. Roslyn sent word to Jesus, "Lord, the man you love is ill." When Jesus arrived in Grand Coteau, he learned that Brennan was in the depths of desolation. (This is true. I was in an agony of indecision. Should Roslyn and I marry? I loved her with all my heart, but the demon of self-deception is subtle. Was it the Father's will for us to marry or my own will? How could I be certain I had heard God's voice? Besides, what does the canon law of the Catholic Church say? And what will *people* say—parents, relatives, friends, the thousands who have heard me preach the Gospel? I was torn up inside, shrouded in darkness and confusion.)

Word was sent to Roslyn, "The teacher is here and asking for you." As soon as she heard this, she got up and started out in His direction. When she came to the place where Jesus was, she fell at His feet and said, "Lord, my

Brennan's heart is broken with grief. He is troubled, confused, and despairing. If You had been here, he would not be like this." Roslyn started to cry. When Jesus saw her weeping, He was troubled in spirit, moved by the deepest emotions. "Where is he?" Jesus asked.

"He is in the chapel. Come, I'll show you where it is." Jesus Himself began to cry. In the distance, some others on retreat whispered, "See how much He loves them."

Jesus approached the chapel and opened the door. "Let us be alone," He said to Roslyn. I was so caught up in my inner turmoil that I didn't notice Him as He came and sat down beside me.

He took my hand. Startled, I turned and looked at Him. He did not say a word. He placed His other hand on top of mine. Then *He smiled.* Oh, how I wish you could have been there! The delight on His face and the merriment in His eyes dispelled every trace of doubt and confusion. In an instant I went from darkest night to sunny noonday. Though He did not speak, His smile spoke: "Do not be afraid. I am with you." I walked out of the chapel feeling like Lazarus emerging from the tomb.

The smiling Christ heals and liberates. With newly discovered delight in ourselves, we go out to our brothers and sisters as we are, where they are, and minister the smiling Christ to them. Not far away from us, there is someone who is afraid and needs our courage; someone who is lonely and needs our presence. There is someone hurt needing our healing; unloved, needing our touching; old, needing to feel that we care; weak, needing the support of our shared weakness. One of the most healing words I ever spoke as a confessor was to an old priest with a drinking problem. "Just a few years ago," I said, "I was a hopeless alcoholic in the gutter in Fort Lauderdale." "You?" he cried. "O thank God!" When we bring a smile to the face of someone in pain, we have brought Christ to them.

Christianity calls for risen Christians, disciples like the hero of Eugene O'Neill's play *Lazarus Laughed*. As mentioned in chapter five, Lazarus has tasted death and seen it for what it is. Now his joy in living is irresistible:

> *Laugh with me!*
> *Death is dead!*
> *Fear is no more!*
> *There is only life!*
> *There is only laughter!*[2]

If darkest night is upon you as you read these words, know that the risen Jesus is wild about you even if you can't feel it. Listen beneath your pain for the voice of Abba God: "Make ready for My Christ whose smile, like lightning, sets free the song of everlasting glory that now sleeps in your paper flesh like dynamite."

Epilogue

In this book I have given license to my language to be what it is: crude and soft-spoken, blunt and compassionate, whole and stricken, honest and provocative, drawn from the casks of life.

The prophetic task of a Christian leader is twofold. First it is to rattle the dead bones in the sanctuary, to expose inauthentic forms of faith, to challenge parochial thinking, to mock false prophets, smash idols, and plunder the strongholds of hypocrisy. Matthew 23 is the prophet's warrant to sting the conscience of the community. Clearly, if he does not first turn his corrective word upon himself, he disqualifies himself as a witness to the Gospel and does the Church a service by keeping his mouth shut. Should the prophet undertake his vocation for any other reason than the love of God and compassion for people, he will communicate nothing but the contagion of his own obsessions and wind up not only a cynic but, as our kids love to chant, "b-o-r-i-n-g."

Second, the prophet also recalls the Church to the purity of the Gospel and the scandal of the cross. Paul confirms in his letters that to follow Jesus is to take the high road to Calvary. Littered along the road will be the skeletons of our egos, the corpses of our fantasies of control, the shards of self-righteousness, self-indulgent spirituality, and unfreedom. The signature of Jesus frees us from bondage to illusion and fear. "On the cross we are liberated to live in truth, in love, in spontaneous responsiveness to the movement of the Spirit in our lives. . . . I have always liked the way John Middleton Murry spoke of such a life, 'For the good man to realize that it is better to be whole than to be good is to enter on a straight and narrow path compared to which his previous rectitude was flowery license.' "[1]

Freedom from the false dependencies discussed in this book—consumerism, hedonism, and domination through violence—is the triumph of the crucified Christ in our lives. To repeat the words of Kasemann quoted earlier: "A man counts as a lover of the Cross only insofar as it enables him to come to terms with himself and others and with the powers and enticements of the world."[2]

The greatest need for our time is for the Church to become what it has seldom been: the *ekklesia* of the Lord Jesus with its face to the world, loving others regardless of religion or culture, pouring itself out in a life of service, offering hope to a frightened world, and presenting itself as a real alternative to the existing arrangement. "The Church that is worthy of the name is a band of people in which the love of God has broken the spell of demons and false gods and which is now making a dent in the world."[3]

I want neither a blood 'n' guts religion that would make

John Wayne, not Jesus, our model, nor an academic religion that would imprison the Gospel in an ivory tower, nor a noisy, feel-good religion that is a naked appeal to emotion. I want passion, intelligence, and love in a church without ostentation, quietly witnessing through the *discipline of the secret*, gently beckoning to the world to come and enjoy the peace and unity we possess because of the Spirit in our midst.

The signature of Jesus is the ultimate expression of God's love for the world. The *ekklesia* is the Church of Jesus Christ only when it is stamped with this signature, only when it faces outward and moves with Him, in community, along the way of the cross. Turned inward upon itself, it loses its identity and its mission.

In the next decade what will separate the committed from the uncommitted will be the depth and quality of our love for Jesus Christ. The superficial will build bigger barns in the euphoria of the prosperity gospel; the trendy will follow the latest fad and try to hum their way to heaven; the defeated will be haunted by ghosts from the past.

And the victorious minority, unintimidated by the cultural patterns of the lockstepping, unbelieving majority will celebrate as though He were near, near in time, near in place, the witness of our motives, our speech, our behavior. As indeed He is.

In the next ten years, God's prophets will call the *ekklesia* to heroism, if not martyrdom. I am reminded of a wonderful scene in Zorba the Greek:

" 'Man, you're not free,' Zorba said. 'The string you're tied to is perhaps longer than other people's. That's all. You're on a long piece of string, boss; you come and go but you never cut the string in two. And when people don't cut that string. . . .'

" 'I'll cut it some day,' I said defiantly. Zorba's words had touched an open wound in me and hurt.

" 'It's difficult, boss, very difficult. You need *a touch of folly* to do that; folly, do you see? You have to risk everything. But you've got such a strong head, it always gets the better of you. A man's head is like a grocer. It keeps accounts. I've paid so much and earned so much and that means a profit of this much or a loss of that much. The head's a careful little shopkeeper; it never risks all it has, always keeps something in reserve. It never breaks the string. Ah, no; it hangs on tight to it. If the string slips out of its grasp, the head, poor devil, is lost, finished. But if a man doesn't break that string, tell me, what flavor is left in life?' "

Zorba is prophetic: it takes a touch of folly to be a disciple; folly, do you see? We have to risk everything.

Perhaps we are all in the position of the man in Morton Kelsey's story who came to the edge of an abyss that he could not cross. As he stood there wondering what to do, he was amazed to discover a tightrope stretched across the abyss. And slowly, surely, across the rope came an acrobat pushing before him a wheelbarrow with another performer in it. When the pair reached the safety of solid ground, the acrobat smiled at the man's amazement. "Do you think I can do it again?" he asked. And the man replied, "Why, yes, I certainly believe you can." The acrobat put his question a second time, and when the answer was the same, he pointed to the wheelbarrow and said, "Good! Then get in and I'll take you across."

What did the man do? In terms of following Jesus, this may be the only question. Do we profess our faith in Him in finely articulated creeds, and then refuse to get into the wheelbarrow? What we *do* about the Lordship of Jesus is a better barometer of our faith than what we think.

In the days head, authentic disciples will be daring enough to be different, humble enough to make mistakes, trusting enough to be burnt in the fire of love, and real enough to make others want to follow.

Lord Jesus Christ, Son of the living God, anoint us with fire. We pray that your Word not only shine in our hearts but that it burn. Goad us and gift us into a daredevil leap into the abyss of Your love. Let the cry of Nikos Kazantzakis arise from our hearts with newborn awareness:

> *I am a bow in your hands, Lord.*
> *Draw me, lest I rot.*
> *Do not overdraw me, Lord, I shall break.*
> *Overdraw me, Lord, and who cares if I break?*

Notes

Chapter 1

1. I am indebted to Alan Jones for his insight on imagination found in *Exploring Spiritual Direction, An Essay on Christian Friendship* (New York: Winston-Seabury Press, 1982). Harned's quote is found on page 84.

2. Found in a parish bulletin.

3. I recommend *Lost Christianity* by Jacob Needleman (New York: Harper & Row, Publishers Inc., 1980).

4. See *The Spirituality of Gentleness* by Judish Lechner (New York: Harper & Row, Publishers Inc., 1987).

5. *Jesus in Focus* by Gerard Sloyan (Philadelphia: Temple University Press, 1983) was helpful here.

6. Jaraslav Pelikan, *Jesus through the Centuries* (New Haven, Conn.: Yale University Press, 1985), p. 155.

7. John Main, *The Present Christ* (New York: The Crossroad Publishing Co., 1986), p. 42.

8. Scott Peck, *The Different Drum* (New York: Simon & Schuster, Inc., 1987), p. 298.

9. Walter Burghardt, *Still Proclaiming Your Wonders* (Mahwah, N.J.: Paulist Press, 1984), p. 228.

10. For a full development of the discipline of the secret, see *Liberating Faith* by Geoffrey B. Kelly (Minneapolis: Augsburg Publishing House, 1984), p. 133 ff.

11. Needleman, p. 119.

12. Larry Rasmussen, "Worship in a World Come-of-Age," in *A Bonheoffer Legacy: Essays in Understanding*, ed. A.J. Klassen (Grand Rapids: Wm. B. Eerdmans Publishing Co., 1981), p. 278.

Chapter 2

1. Jurgen Moltmann, *The Crucified God* (New York: Harper & Row, Publishers Inc., 1974), p. 154.

2. Ernst Kasemann, *Jesus Means Freedom* (Philadelphia: Fortress Press, 1969), p. 176.

3. Robert Bolt, *A Man for All Seasons* (New York: Random House Inc., 1960), p. 140.

4. John Shea, *The Challenge of Jesus* (Chicago: The Thomas More Press, 1984), p. 178.

5. Jim Wallis, *The Call to Conversion* (New York: Harper & Row, Publishers Inc., 1981), p. 43.

Chapter 3

1. Walter Wink, *Unmasking the Powers: The Invisible Forces that Determine Human Existence* (Philadelphia: Fortress Press, 1986), p. 105.

2. John Kavanaugh, S.J., gave a splendid address on radical Christianity at Fordham University in August 1985. In this chapter I have quoted from his paper and applied his ideas to the theme of the chapter.

3. Thomas Merton, *The Hidden Ground of Love* (New York: Farrar, Straus & Giroux, Inc., 1985), p. 112.

4. John McKenzie, *The Civilization of Christianity* (Chicago: The Thomas More Press, 1986), p. 66.

5. "Profiles and Personalities," *People magazine* (March 9, 1987).

6. McKenzie, p. 56.

7. McKenzie, p. 242.

8. Kavanaugh, p. 9.

9. Mark Twain, *The War Prayer* (New York: Harper & Row, Publishers Inc., 1984), quoted in McKenzie, p. 127.

10. Merton, p. 211.

11. Kavanaugh, p. 12.

12. Parker J. Palmer, *The Promise of Paradox*, A Celebration of Contradictions in the Christian Life (Notre Dame, Ind.: Ave Maria Press, 1980), p. 81.

13. Peck, p. 233.

14. Wallis, p. 178.

Chapter 4

1. Thomas N. Hart, *To Know and Follow Jesus* (Mahwah, N.J.: Paulist Press, 1985), p. 33. This is an excellent study in contemporary Christology. It is highly readable and highly recommended. ·

2. Thomas R. Kelly, *A Testament of Devotion* (New York: Harper & Row, Publishers Inc., 1941), p. 58.

3. Kelly, p. 53.

4. Donald P. Gray, *Jesus, the Way to Freedom* (Winona, Minn.: St. Mary's Press, 1979), p. 38. This little 72-page book is scholarly but not obtuse. It breathes the freedom of the Gospel. If you are going to read one other book on Jesus this year, I suggest this one.

5. Keith Miller, *The Scent of Love* (Waco, Tex.: Word Books, 1983), quoted in Peck, p. 294.

6. Strob Talbot, "Ethics in the Corporate World," *Time* (May 25, 1987).

7. Kelly, p. 114.

Chapter 5

1. William J. Bausch, *Storytelling, Imagination and Faith* (Mystic, Conn.: Twenty-Third Publications, 1984), p. 141.

2. John Heagle, *On the Way* (Chicago: The Thomas More Press, 1981), p. 34.

3. Raymond Brown, *The Churches the Apostles Left Behind* (Mahwah, N.J.: Paulist Press, 1984), p. 91.

4. Bausch, p. 29.

5. Eugene Kennedy, *The Choice to Be Human: Jesus Alive in the Gospel of Matthew* (New York: Doubleday & Co., Inc., 1985), p. 130.

6. Rodgers & Hammerstein, "My Favorite Things," *The Sound of Music* (1960).

7. Peck, p. 295.

8. Martin Marty, *Context, A Commentary on the Interaction of Religion and Culture* (Chicago: Claretian Publications, 1987), p. 5.

9. Burkhardt, p. 168.

10. See *Certain as the Dawn* by Peter van Breman (Denville, N.J.: Dimension Books, 1980).

11. Heagle, p. 210.

Chapter 6

1. Anthony DeMello, S.J., *The Song of the Bird* (Anand, India: Gujarat Sahitya Prakash, distributed by Loyola University Press, Chicago, 1983), p. 130.

2. Thomas Merton, *The Hidden Ground of Love* (New York: Farrar, Straus & Giroux, Inc., 1986). Letter to Daniel Berrigen, March 10, 1968.

3. Anthony Bloom and Georges LeFevre, *The Courage to Pray* (Mahwah, N.J.: Paulist Press, 1973), p. 17.

4. DeMello, p. 134.

5. Alan Jones, *Soul Making, The Desert Way of Spirituality* (New York: Harper & Row, Publishers Inc., 1985), p. 177.

6. Jones, p. 178.

7. Merton. This quote is from a letter to Dom Francois Decroix, April 21, 1967.

8. Hans Küng, *On Being a Christian* (New York: Doubleday & Co., Inc., 1976), pp. 341–342. Used by permission.

Chapter 7

1. Walter J. Burghardt, S.J., *Still Proclaiming Your Wonders* (Mahwah, N.J.: Paulist Press, 1984), p. 140.

2. Andrew Canale, *Understanding the Human Jesus* (Mahwah, N.J.: Paulist Press, 1985), p. 35. With an introduction by Morton Kelsey, this is a fine journey in Scripture and imagination.

3. Canale, p. 35.

4. Raymond Brown, *Son of God, Son of Man* (New York: Doubleday & Co., Inc., 1976), p. 147.

5. Peter van Breeman, *Called by Name* (Denville, N.J.: Dimension Books, 1976), p. 43.

6. Peter van Breeman, *As Bread that Is Broken* (Denville, N.J.: Dimension Books, 1974), p. 28.

7. Anthony DeMello, *Sadhana, A Way to God* (New York: Doubleday & Co., Inc., 1978), p. 182.

Chapter 8

1. Anthony DeMello, S.J., *The Song of the Bird* (Anand, India: Gujarat Sahitya Prakash, distributed by Loyola University Press, Chicago, 1983), pp. 190–191.

2. Excerpt from an essay in theological studies by Walter Burghardt that I noted years ago. The title of the essay and the date of publication are unavailable to me.

3. Walter J. Burghardt, *Tell the Next Generation* (Mahwah, N.J.: Paulist Press, 1980), p. 51.

4. Ralph Martin, *Fire on the Earth* (New York: Doubleday & Co., Inc., 1983), p. 64.

5. Parker J. Palmer, *The Promise of Paradox* (Notre Dame, Ind.: Ave Maria Press, 1980), p. 56.

6. Thomas N. Hart, *To Know and Follow Jesus* (Mahwah, N.J.: Paulist Press, 1985), p. 136.

7. Hart, p. 139.

8. Hart, p. 139.

9. Walter Burghardt, *Grace on Crutches* (Mahwah, N.J.: Paulist Press, 1986), p. 102.

10. Hart, p. 135.

11. Thomas Stransky, "The Salvation of Non-Christians," *America* (March 1986), p. 18.

12. James T. Burtchaell, *Philemon's Problem* (Chicago: ACTA Foundation, 1973), p. 44.

13. Hart, p. 143.

14. Palmer, p. 51.

Chapter 9

1. Alan Jones, *Exploring Spiritual Direction* (New York: Winston-Seabury Press, 1982), p. 115.

2. Tim Hansel, *You Gotta Keep Dancin'* (Elgin, Ill.: David C. Cook Publishing Co., 1985), p. 48.

3. The insight into this parable came from Christian psychologist and friend Molly Clark of Bastrop, La.

4. Myles Connolly, *Mister Blue* (New York: Macmillan Publishing Co., 1928), p. 91.

5. Jones, p. 39.

Chapter 10

1. Sharon Begley, "The Big Bang," *Newsweek* (March 12, 1979), p. 36.

2. William E. Reiser, *Into the Needle's Eye* (Notre Dame, Ind.: Ave Maria Press, 1984), p. 86.

3. Brother David Steindl-Rast, *Gratefulness, the Heart of Prayer* (Mahwah, N.J.: Paulist Press, 1984), p. 64.

4. Basil Pennington, *Centering Prayer* (New York: Doubleday & Co., Inc., 1980), pp. 68–69.

5. John Main, *The Present Christ* (New York: The Crossroad Publishing Co., 1985), p. 3.

Chapter 11

1. Walter Burghardt, *Tell the Next Generation* (Mahwah, N.J.: Paulist Press, 1980), p. 125.

2. Burghardt, p. 48.

Epilogue

1. Parker J. Palmer, *The Promise of Paradox* (Notre Dame, Ind.: Ave Maria Press, 1980), p. 28.

2. Ernst Kasemann, *Jesus Means Freedom* (Philadelphia: Fortress Press, 1969), p. 76.

3. Kasemann, p. 77.